Power System Interview Questions & Answers

DR. SOUDAMINI BEHERA

Made with ❤ on the Notion Press Platform

www.notionpress.com

This Book is dedicated to my husband Mr. Debabrata Behera, my lovely kids Yoddha and Yash

Acknowledgments

This acknowledgement is dedicated to those people, who's beautiful, creative and unpretentious mind has made my journey worthwhile calling an experience.

I must express my very profound gratitude to my parents Mr. Nanda Kishore Behera and Mrs. Anupama Behera, parents-in-law Mr. Jugal Kishore Behera and late Mrs. Jamini Behera, husband Mr. Debabrata Behera, my lovely kids Yoddha and Yash for imparting me with unfailing help and non-stop encouragement during the journey of writing the book. This accomplishment could now no longer have been viable without them. Thanks to them who have extended the whole-hearted support during the days of my research work.

Power System Interview Questions-Set 1

1) What is the Power plant or Power Station?

The power plant refers to the network that is made up of the generation, distribution, and transmission systems. Electricity is produced by the power plant by utilising fuels like coal and diesel. A grid providing electricity to another system is an illustration of a power system.

2) What do you mean by the zone of protection?

The power system is designed with protection for every single component. The system's relays trip all circuit breakers in the event of a fault, removing the problematic component from the power system. Known as the "Zone of Protection," this level of system security is offered.

3) What is the difference between the Transmission line and distribution line?

Transferring power from one location to another is the primary function of both distribution and transmission lines. However, there are some key differences between the two types of lines, including the type of phase, the thickness of the wire used in the distribution line compared to the transmission line's thin wire, and the requirement for a single phase supply for distribution lines versus a three phase supply for transmission lines.

4) What are the common sources of energy?

The common sources of energy are:

- Sun.
- Water.
- Water head.
- Fuel.
- Nuclear Energy.

5) Write down the classification of the transmission line?

The transmission line is classified as follows based on the conductor's length and voltage:

1. A.C Transmission Line.

- Short transmission line.
- Medium transmission line.
    - Pi model of a medium transmission line.
    - T model of a medium transmission line.
- Long transmission line.

2. D.C Transmission Line.

6) What is a Relay?

Relays are automatic devices that sense abnormalities in electrical circuits and shut off their contacts.

7) How many types of Protection relays are there based on the Characteristic?

On the basis of a characteristic, protection relays can be categorized as follows:

- Definite time relays.
- IDMT (Inverse time relays with definite minimum time).
- Instantaneous relays.
- IDMT with inst.
- Stepped Characteristic relays.
- Programmed Characteristic relays.
- Voltage Restraint overcurrent relays.

8) What is meant by Reset level of the Relay?

The reset level of a relay is the current or voltage below which the relay opens its contact.

9) What are the internal and external faults?

Faults that happen outside the protective zone are known as external faults, and faults that happen inside the zone are known as internal faults.

10) How many types of faults are there in 3 phase power system?

The faults that occur in the three-phase power system are as follows:

- Single line to ground (LG) fault
- Line to line (LL) fault
- Double line to ground (LLG) fault
- Three Phase short circuit (LLL) fault
- Three phase to ground (LLLG) fault

11) What do you mean by reach and reach the point of the relay?

Reach is the distance between the reach point and relay, and the reach point is the location that is furthest from the relay while it is still within the protective zone.

12) Why does the adjacent zone of protection overlap?

There should be overlap in the adjacent zone of protection because otherwise, some part of the power system will remain exposed and unprotected.

13) What is Electrical Grounding?

The safety precaution of electrical grounding, or just grounding, keeps people from unintentionally coming into contact with potentially dangerous electrical faults.

14) What is Electrical Earthing?

The process of immediately discharging electrical energy to the earth with the use of low resistance wire is known as electrical earthing.

15) How many types of electrical earthing are there?

Electrical earthing is of two types:

1. Neutral Earthing.
2. Equipment Earthing.

16) What is the difference between Electrical earthing and Electrical grounding?

Electrical earthing and electrical grounding are not the same thing. Earthing involves connecting the non-current carrying part of an electrical system to the ground, while grounding involves connecting the current carrying part to the ground. Although earthing has zero potential, grounding does not.

17) What is the importance of earthing?

Earthing is crucial for the reasons listed below:

1. The person is shielded from the short circuit current by earthing.
2. When insulation fails, earthing offers the simplest route for short-circuit current to flow.

3. Earthing shields people and equipment from lightning discharge and high voltage surges.

18) What is meant by Sag?

The level difference between the conductor's lowest point and its points of support is known as "sag."

19) What is Corona?

The violet glow, hissing sound, and ozone gas production in an overhead gearbox line are all known as the **"Corona"** phenomenon.

20) Draw the Single Line Diagram of the Power Station?

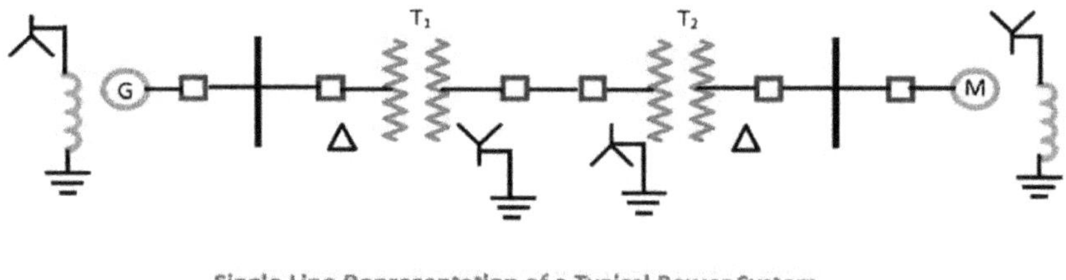

Single Line Representation of a Typical Power System

21) How do you select the pickup value of the relay?

Relays must have pickup values greater than the maximum load in order to supply both the normal load and a certain amount of overload. The pickup value should be less than the smallest fault current because the relay should be sensitive enough to react to even the smallest fault.

22) What is the difference between a fuse and a breaker?

A fuse operates on the thermal and electrical characteristics of conducting materials, whereas a circuit breaker operates on the principles of electromagnetism and switching. This is the difference between a fuse and a circuit breaker. Fuse breaking capacity is lower than circuit breaker breaking capacity, and we can only use fuses once while circuit breakers can be used repeatedly.

23) What is the difference between the relay and the circuit breaker?

Relays are switching devices that send signals to circuit breakers when faults occur, but circuit breakers automatically cut the circuit when they receive a signal. This is how relays and circuit breakers differ from one another.

24) What is the difference between resistance grounding system and resistance earthing system?

One or more resistances are connected to the system's neutral in resistance grounding. Resistance winding shields the system from transient overvoltages and restricts the fault current. Resistance earthing reduces the risk of arcing on the ground and allows for ground fault protection; on the other hand, resistance earthing systems are installed in electric equipment to safeguard it against system faults.

25) What is Primary and Backup protection?

Primary protection, sometimes referred to as main protection, is the first line of defence that offers prompt fault acting and clearing inside the protected elements' boundaries. Every section of the electrical installation has primary protection. On the other hand, backup protection acts as a fallback for the primary or main protection in the event that it malfunctions and needs to be repaired. Backup protection is necessary for the electrical system to operate properly.

26) What is meant by Bus Bar Protection?

When a bus bar fault arises, the entire supply is disrupted, and all feeders are disconnected. In this scenario, the system is equipped with busbar protection to prevent future occurrences of these faults. The circuits connecting the faulty section must all be open in order to remove the faults.

27) How many types of fault occur in a 3-phase power system?

Voltage and current deviations from standard values are known as electrical faults. In three-phase systems, there are two kinds of faults that can happen.

1. Symmetrical faults.
2. Unsymmetrical faults.

28) What are the effects of Electrical Faults?

The effects of electrical faults are as follows:

1. **Overcurrent flow**- When a fault occurs, the system experiences high current flows, which cause relays to trip and damage insulation and equipment components.
2. **The danger to operating personnel**- The person working there may also be impacted by the fault, and the voltage and current at the fault site determine how serious the fault is.
3. **Loss of equipment**- Heavy current due to short circuit faults result in the burning of equipment completely which leads to improper working of equipment or device.
4. **Disturbed interconnected active circuits**- During the occurrence of fault the active, connected components of the system also get disturbed.

29) Give some example of fault limiting devices?

Some examples of fault limiting devices are as follows:

1. **Circuit Breaker**- When an abnormal condition arises, the device breaks. It functions normally otherwise.
2. **Fuse-**A fuse is a fundamental safety device that consists of a small wire connected to two metal pieces, covered by a casing or glass.
3. **Relay**- This switch operates on a conditional basis, opening its contact in response to an abnormal condition.
4. **Lighting power protection devices**- These include grounding devices and lightning arrestors, which are used to shield the system from lightning strikes or surge voltages.

30) When are the directional relays used?

Directional relays are used in a single end fed system of parallel feeders in the ring main feeder system.

31) What are the causes of electrical faults?

The causes of electrical faults are as follows:

1. The current weather, which includes lightning strikes, torrential rain, strong winds, salt build up on overhead wires and other conductors, etc., disrupts the power supply and deteriorates electrical installations.
2. Equipment such as transformers, motors, and generators fail due to insulation failure, ageing, and malfunctioning cables and windings.
3. Human error can also result in electrical faults. Examples of this include choosing equipment with the incorrect rating or flipping the circuit while it is being serviced.

32) What is Skin Effect?

The term "Skin Effect" refers to the tendency of an alternating electric current (A.C.) to be distributed within a conductor so that the current density increases close to the conductor's surface and decreases with increasing conductor depth.

33) What is the bundle conductor?

Two or more parallel sub conductors spaced several diameters apart make up a bundle conductor.

34) What is the use of bundle conductors?

The use of bundle conductors lessens the influence of the skin and corona.

35) What are the commonly used schemes for the bus zone protection?

The commonly used schemes for the protection are:

- Backup Protection.
- Differential overcurrent protection.
- Circulating current protection.
- Voltage overvoltage protection.
- Frame leakage protection.

36) What are the internal and external faults?

Faults that happen inside the protective zone are known as internal faults, and faults that happen outside the protective zone are known as external faults.

37) What are the advantages of a Three-Phase system over a Single-Phase System?

The following are the benefits of a three-phase transformer over a single-phase transformer:

1. Power delivery in a single-phase system is pulsating, while power delivery in a three-phase system is constant.
2. Induction motors with three phases are more efficient and self-starting than those with one phase, which need an additional source of power to initiate.
3. For a given frame size, the three-phase machine produces more than a single-phase machine does.
4. Single phase motors have a low power factor while three phase motors have a higher power factor.

38) What is Critical disruptive Voltage?

The critical disruptive voltage is the lowest phase to a neutral voltage needed to initiate a corona discharge. The air current discharge is referred to in this context as the corona discharge.

Critical Disruptive Voltage:

$Vc = \mu \times \beta \times [r \log (d/r)]$

In the case of a distinct surface condition, the value of the surface irregularity factor μ is as follows:

Surface Condition	Value of Surface Irregularity Factor μ
Polished Surface	1
Conductor with dust deposit	0.92 to 0.98
Stranded Conductor	0.8 to 0.87

39) What is a Slack bus?

A slack bus also known as reference bus or swing bus balances the active and reactive power of the system. The slack bus serves as angular reference for all the buses in the system.

40) How many methods use the load flow solution?

The method that uses the load flow analysis is as follows:

- Gauss-Seidel method using Y bus
- Newton- Raphson method (NR)
- Power flow through slack bus and line.
- Decouple load flow method
- Fast Decouple load flow method.

Power System Interview Questions and Answers -Set 2

1) What is the Power plant or Power Station?

The generation, distribution, and transmission system together constitute a network called as Power plant. The power plant uses the form of energy such as coal, diesel and converts it into electrical energy. An example of the power system is a grid that supplies power to the other system.

2) What do you mean by the zone of protection?

The protection is provided in the system to protect each and every element of the power system. If any fault occurs in the system, then the relays associated with it trip all the circuit breaker so that the faulty element gets removed from the power system. This Security provided to the system is called the 'Zone of protection'.

3) What is the difference between the Transmission line and distribution line?

The main work of transmission line and distribution line is to transfer power from one place to another but the difference between transmission and distribution line is based on the factors like the type of phase, the distribution line because the wire for transmission line is thick and for distribution line is thin, the transmission line requires three phase supply for carrying electricity and distribution line requires single phase supply for carrying electricity.

4) What are the common sources of energy?

The common sources of energy are:

- Sun.
- Water.
- Waterhead.
- Fuel.
- Nuclear Energy.

5) Write down the classification of the transmission line?

Depending upon the voltage and length of the conductor the classification of the transmission line is as follows:

1. A.C Transmission Line.

- Short transmission line.
- Medium transmission line.
  - Pi model of a medium transmission line.
  - T model of a medium transmission line.
- Long transmission line.

2. D.C Transmission Line.

6) What is a Relay?

The Relay is an automatic device that senses the abnormal condition of the electrical circuit and closes its contact.

7) How many types of Protection relays are there based on the Characteristic?

On the basis of a characteristic, protection relays can be categorized as follows:

- Definite time relays.
- IDMT (Inverse time relays with definite minimum time).
- Instantaneous relays.
- IDMT with inst.
- Stepped Characteristic relays.
- Programmed Characteristic relays.
- Voltage Restraint overcurrent relays.
-

8) What is meant by Reset level of the Relay?

The value of current or voltage below which the relay opens it contact is called the reset level of the relay.

9) What are the internal and external faults?

Internal faults are the faults that occur inside the zone and external faults are the faults that occur outside the zone of protection.

10) How many types of faults are there in 3 phase power system?

The faults that occur in the three-phase power system are as follows:

1. Single line to ground (LG) fault
2. Line to line (LL) fault
3. Double line to ground (LLG) fault
4. Three Phase short circuit (LLL) fault
5. Three phase to ground (LLLG) fault

11) What do you mean by reach and reach the point of the relay?

The reach point is the farthest point from the relay which is still inside the zone of protection and reach is the distance between the reach point and relay.

12) Why does the adjacent zone of protection overlap?

Adjacent zone of protection overlap because if we do not overlap then some portion of the power system will be left out unprotected.

13) What is Electrical Grounding?

Electrical grounding or merely grounding is a safety measure used to prevent people accidentally coming in contact with the hazardous electrical faults.

14) What is Electrical Earthing?

Electrical earthing is a process of transferring the immediate discharge of the electrical energy directly to the earth by the help of low resistance wire.

15) How many types of electrical earthing are there?

Electrical earthing is of two types:

1. Neutral Earthing.
2. Equipment Earthing.

16) What is the difference between Electrical earthing and Electrical grounding?

The difference between electrical earthing and electrical grounding is that in grounding the current carrying part is connected to the ground, whereas in earthing the non-current carrying part is connected to the ground. Grounding does not have zero potential but earthing has zero potential.

17) What is the importance of earthing?

- Earthing is important because of the given below reasons: Earthing protects the person from the short circuit current.
- Earthing provides the easiest path of flow for short-circuit current at the time of insulation failure.
- Earthing protects the persons and apparatus from the high voltage surges and lightning discharge.

18) What is meant by Sag?

'Sag' is the difference in level between the points of support and the lowest point on the conductor.

19) What is Corona?

'Corona' is the phenomenon of violet glow, hissing noise, and production of ozone gas in an overhead transmission line.

20) How do you select the pickup value of the relay?

The pickup value of the relay should be more than the maximum load and it should allow the normal load as well as the certain degree of overload to be supplied. The relay should be sensitive enough to respond to the smallest fault, therefore, the pickup value should be less than the smallest fault current.

21) What is the difference between a fuse and a breaker?

The difference between Fuse and a circuit breaker is that fuse works on the principle of the thermal and electrical properties of the conducting materials, whereas the circuit breaker works on the principle of electromagnetism and switching principle. We can use the fuses only once but circuit breakers can be used many more times, and the breaking capacity of the fuse is low as compared with the circuit breaker.

22) What is the difference between the relay and the circuit breaker?

The difference between the relay and the circuit breaker is that relay is a switching device that gives the signal to the circuit breaker in case of fault occurrence, whereas circuit breaker breaks the circuit automatically when receives the signal.

23) What is the difference between resistance grounding system and resistance earthing system?

In resistance grounding, one or more resistance is connected to the neutral of the system. Resistance winding limits the fault current and protects the system from transient over voltages. The arcing ground risk is decreased by the resistance grounding and permits the ground fault protection, whereas resistance earthing system is provided in electric equipment to protect the equipment from the occurrence of the fault in the system.

24) What is Primary and Backup protection?

Primary protection also known as main protection is the first line of protection which provides quick acting and clearing of the fault within the boundary of the elements it protects. In the electrical installation, the primary protection is provided to each section. Whereas the backup protection provides the backup to the primary or main protection whenever it fails in operation and cut out for repair. For the proper functioning of the electrical system back up protection is essential.

25) What is meant by Bus Bar Protection?

When the fault occurs on the bus bar, then the whole of the supply gets interrupted, and all the feeders are disconnected in this case Busbar protection is provided to the system to eliminate the occurrence of these faults. For removing the faults the entire circuits connecting the faulty section needs to be open.

26) How many types of fault occur in a 3-phase power system?

Electrical faults are the deviation of voltage and current from normal values. There are two types of faults that occur in a three-phase system.

- Symmetrical faults.
- Unsymmetrical faults.

27) What are the effects of Electrical Faults?

The effects of electrical faults are as follows:

- Overcurrent flow- During fault occurrence high current flows in the system and which leads to tripping of relays, damaging insulation and components of the equipment.
- The danger to operating personnel- Fault can also affect the individual working there, and severity of the fault depends upon the voltage and current at the point of fault.
- Loss of equipment- Heavy current due to short circuit faults result in the burning of equipment completely which leads to improper working of equipment or device.
- Disturbed interconnected active circuits- During the occurrence of fault the active, connected components of the system also get disturbed.

28) Give some example of fault limiting devices?

Some examples of fault limiting devices are as follows:

- Circuit Breaker- It is a device which works in normal condition and breaks when an abnormal condition occurs.
- Fuse- A fuse is a thin wire enclosed in a casing or glass which connects two metal parts. It is used as a primary protection device.
- Relay- It is a condition based operating switch which opens its contact when an abnormal condition occurs.
- Lighting power protection devices- These are the devices that are used to protect the system from surge voltages or lighting like- lightning arrestors and grounding devices.

29) When are the directional relays used?

In ring main feeder system, single end fed system of parallel feeders directional relays are used.

30) What are the causes of electrical faults?

The causes of electrical faults are as follows:

- The existing weather conditions like lightning strikes, heavy rains, heavy winds, salt deposition on overhead lines and conductors etc. interrupts the powers supply and damages the damages the electrical installations.
- Malfunctioning, aging, insulation failure of cables and winding leads to failure of equipment like generators, motor, transformer.
- Electrical faults are also caused because of human errors such as selecting an improper rating of equipment, switching the circuit while it is under servicing etc.

31) What is Skin Effect?

The tendency of an alternating electric current (A.C) to get distributed within a conductor such that the current density becomes largest near the surface of the conductor, and decreases with greater depth in the conductor, is called as "Skin Effect."

32) What is the bundle conductor?

A bundle conductor consists of two or more parallel sub conductors at a spacing of several diameters.

33) What is the use of bundle conductors?

Bundle conductors are used to reducing the Corona and Skin effect.

34) What are the commonly used schemes for the bus zone protection?

The commonly used schemes for the protection are:

- Backup Protection.
- Differential overcurrent protection.
- Circulating current protection.
- Voltage overvoltage protection.
- Frame leakage protection.

35) What are the internal and external faults?

Internal faults are the faults that occur within the zone of protection and external faults are the faults that occur outside the zone of protection.

36) What are the advantages of a Three-Phase system over a Single-Phase System?

The advantages of the three-phase transformer over a single-phase transformer are as follows:

- In the three-phase system, the power delivered is constant whereas the power delivered in the single-phase system is pulsating in nature.
- The three-phase induction motors are self-starting and more efficient whereas the single-phase motor is not self-starting and requires an auxiliary means for the start of motor.
- The output of the three-phase machine is higher than a single-phase machine for a given size of a frame.
- Three phase motors have higher power factor whereas the single phase motors have low power factor.

37) What is Critical disruptive Voltage?

The minimum phase to a neutral voltage that is required for corona discharge to start is called the Critical disruptive voltage. In this, the corona discharge means the current discharge in the air.

Critical Disruptive Voltage:

Vc = μ x ß x[r log (d/r)]

Where the value of surface irregularity factor μ for a different surface condition is as follows:

Surface Condition Value of Surface Irregularity Factor μ

Polished Surface 1

Conductor with dust deposit 0.92 to 0.98

Stranded Conductor 0.8 to 0.87

39) What is a Slack bus?

A slack bus also known as reference bus or swing bus balances the active and reactive power of the system. The slack bus serves as angular reference for all the buses in the system.

40) How many methods use the load flow solution?

The method that uses the load flow analysis is as follows:

- Gauss-Seidel method using Y bus
- Newton- Raphson method (NR)
- Power flow through slack bus and line.
- Decouple load flow method
- Fast Decouple load flow method.

Power System Interview Question and Answers- Set 3

1) What is meant by synchronous condenser?

An over excited synchronous motor running on no load is known as synchronous condenser. It is used to improve the power factor of the system.

2) Define Power Factor.

The cosine of angle between voltage and the current in an AC circuit is known as power factor.

The value of power factor will always be less than 1.

It is a usual practice to attach a word lagging or leading with the numerical value of power factor to signify whether the current lags or leads the voltage.

3) What is the difference between fuse and circuit breaker?

(i) Fuse performs both detection and interruption functions. Circuit breaker performs interruption function only. The detection of fault is made by relay system.

(ii) The breaking capacity of fuse is very small compare to that of circuit breaker.

(iii) The operating time of the fuse is smaller than operating time of CB.

(iv) After every operation, replacement is required in the fuse. In case of circuit breaker, replacement is not required.

4) What is meant by Sag?

The difference in level between points of supports and the lowest point on the conductor is called sag.

5) What is corona?

The phenomenon of violet glow, hissing noise and production of ozone gas in an overhead transmission line is known as corona.

6) How can we reduce the effect of corona?

1. By increasing conductor size:

By increasing conductor size, the voltage at which corona occurs is raised and hence corona effects are considerably reduced.

2. By increasing conductor spacing:

By increasing the spacing between conductors, the voltage at which corona occurs is raised and hence corona effects can be eliminated.

7) What is tariff?

The rate at which electrical energy is supplied to a consumer is known as tariff.

The tariff should include the following items:

(i) Recovery of cost of producing electrical energy at the power station

(ii) Recovery of cost on the capital investment in transmission and distribution systems.

(iii) Recovery of cost of operation and maintenance of supply

(iv) A suitable profit on the capital investment.

8) What are the various types of tariff?

1.Simple tariff
2.Flat rate tariff
3. Block rate tariff
4. Two-part tariff

5. Maximum demand tariff

6. Power factor tariff

7. Three-part tariff

9) What are the advantages and disadvantages of nuclear power plant?

Advantages:

(i) The amount of fuel required is quite small.

(ii) It requires less space so it can be located near to the load centre.

(iii) Huge deposits of nuclear fuels available all over the world. So supply of electricity can be ensured.

(iv) It ensures reliability of operation.

Disadvantages:

(i)The fuel used is expensive and is difficult to recover.

(ii) The capital cost on a nuclear plant is very high as compared to other types of plants

(iii) The disposal of the by-products is a big problem. They are radioactive in nature.

(iv) The maintenance charges are high.

Power System Interview Questions and Answers -Set 4

1) What is Power System?

The Power system is a system that is made up of the components that are used in the Distribution, Generation, and Transmission systems. The power system serves to create electrical energy by using coal and diesel as inputs. The system is equipped with components such as a

- Motor,
- Circuit breaker,
- Synchronous generator,
- Transformer, and
- Conductor, among other things.

2) What is meant by P-V curves?

- P is an abbreviation for pressure,
- V is an abbreviation for volume

in the P-V curve.

A PV curve or indication diagram displays the proportional change in pressure & volume that occurs inside a system.

This curve is very helpful in a variety of processes, including thermodynamics, respiratory physiology, and cardiovascular physiology. The P-V curve was developed in the eighteenth century in order to have a better understanding of efficient engines.

3) What does "synchronous condenser" mean?

Synchronous Condenser, also known as Synchronous Phase Modifier (or) Synchronous Compensator, is a sophisticated method for increasing power factor. This is a motor that operates without the need of a mechanical load. By altering the field winding's excitation. The reactive volt ampere may be absorbed or generated by a synchronous condenser.

For power factor improvements more than 500 KVAR, a synchronous condenser is preferable than a static condenser.

For lower-rated systems, a capacitor bank is employed.

4) What is the difference between a fuse and a circuit breaker?

Fuse	**Circuit Breaker**
A fuse is a wire that keeps a circuit from overheating. It does not imply overload.	A circuit breaker is an automatic switch that protects a circuit against overloading.
It does not denote overloads.	It denotes overloads.
It can only be used once.	It may be used several times.
It protects against power overloads.	It protects against not just power overloads but additionally short circuits.
It is incapable of detecting fault circuit conditions. It merely executes the interruption procedure.	It detects and interrupts defective circuit conditions.
It has a low breaking strength.	In compared to the fuse, it has a higher breaking capability.
It operates automatically.	Circuit breakers may be either automated or manual.

It operates in a very short period of time, around 0.002 seconds.	It operates in 0.02-0.05 seconds.
It is less expensive than a circuit breaker.	It is expensive.

5) What is referred as tariff?

Tariff refers to the charge levied on items imported from other nations in order to make them more expensive. As a consequence, product costs rise and become less desired or competitive in comparison to local goods and services. Tariffs are imposed to limit commerce from certain foreign nations or to reduce imports of a specific product.

The government imposes two different types of tariffs:

- Tariff Specification
- Ad-valorem Tariff

6) What is the difference between a transmission & distribution line?

Transmission lines are utilised across long distances and have greater voltage to transfer more power. In other terms, the transmission line transfers power from the power plants to the substations.

Distribution lines deliver power across small distances. They can transfer power locally since the voltage is lower. The substation supplies power to the residences.

7) What are the different types of energy sources?

There are only two categories of energy sources,

- Renewable Energy Source
- Non-Renewable Energy Source

which are further subdivided:

Renewable Energy Source – The energy sources originate from a natural source that is refreshed constantly.

The following are examples of renewal sources:

- Solar energy
- Wind energy
- Geothermal energy
- Water energy
- Biomass and biofuels energy

Non-Renewable Energy Source-The energy depleted from a source that cannot be restored and will eventually run out. Non-renewable energy source includes

- Oil
- Coal
- Petroleum and
- Natural Gas

8) What is the function of relay?

The switches that close and open the circuit are referred to as relays. They carry out this duty both electrically and electromechanically. Relays are employed in a variety of applications, including manufacturing. To manage the electricity, control panels & building automation are used.

Relay Types: Relays are classified into many types based on their operating principles. polarity and operation:

- Electromechanical Relay
- Solid State Relay
- Electro thermal Relay

- Electromagnetic relay
- Hybrid Relay

9) What is a nuclear power plant?

Nuclear power plants employ nuclear fission to create energy. Nuclear reactors and the Rankine cycle (which converts water into steam) are used to produce heat. This steam is needed to power the turbine & generator. Nuclear power accounts for 11% of total global electricity production.

The following is a list of the components used in nuclear power reactors to create energy.

- Steam Generation
- Nuclear Reactor
- Turbine & Generator
- Water Cooling Towers

10) What is mean by cable grading or grading of cables?

The term "grading of cable" refers to the process of achieving a uniform distribution of dielectric stress (or) voltage gradient in a dielectric. The dielectric stress is at its absolute lowest at the conductor's outermost sheath, while it is at its absolute greatest near the surface.

Because the tension is not distributed evenly across the cable, the insulation will eventually break down, which will result in the cable becoming thicker. The grading of cables is that allows for the uniform distribution of dielectric stress, which allows for this problem to be circumvented.

11) What is a pumped storage plant?

Pumped-storage hydroelectricity, commonly known as hydroelectricity, is a kind of hydroelectric energy storage that is used for load balancing. When there is a significant demand for electricity, the reservoir's water is discharged via turbines to create electricity. It has the most storage capacity available for the grid.

12) How to verify current transformer(**CT**)**?**

A digital multimeter equipped with a millivolt AC (mV_{ac}) range may be used to evaluate the output voltage (V_o) of a current transformer (CT) out in the field. This test is helpful for confirming that the CT is functioning correctly that current flows through the conductor on which the CT is mounted.

13) What is ACSR?

ACSR – Aluminium Conductor Steel-Reinforced Cable

The term "aluminium conductor steel-reinforced cable" (ACSR) refers to a specific kind of stranded conductor that has a high capacity and a high strength and is often used in overhead power lines. Aluminium of very high purity is used for the outer strands because of the material's excellent conductivity, low weight, cheap cost, resistance to corrosion, and reasonable mechanical stress resistance.

14) Describe the Ferranti effect

The voltage increases at a transmission lines of receiver end compared to the sending end voltage is known as the Ferranti effect. It is seen when there is either no load connected or a very modest load.

15) What is Internal and External faults?

Internal Faults

- Phase-to-phase faults that are internal in nature lead to system component failure.
- Overheating and failed windings may lead to internal defects.
- The cooling system's failure may potentially result in a mechanical issue.

The most effective way to prevent internal defects is via testing and maintenance.

External Faults

- An external failure happens outside the transformer or system. It does not include defective hardware.

- Damage may result from external issues like lightning strikes.
- It is a defect even if the air temperature is higher than a threshold value.

Since these conditions are unpredictable, the problem can only be fixed after the underlying cause has disappeared.

Therefore, it is crucial to be ready for these types of circumstances. External faults are minimal, but if the issue is not fixed, the system might fail.

16) What is meant by electrical grounding and earthing?

Grounding

Grounding may be used to obtain insulation against unintentional currents. The main wire is attached to the power source, while a separate section of the cable is tucked inside the mattress. Overloading and other harmful consequences are avoided.

Earthing

Because these unplanned surges and bursts of electricity pose a risk to human life, earthing is utilised to defend against them. Connecting an earth wire from equipment to the ground allows for earthing. An extremely low resistance channel for the passage of electricity to ground is provided by earth wire. A person won't experience the shock as a result.

17) What is Sag?

The distance between the highest point of a pair of electric poles or towers from the lowest point of the conductor that connects those two points is called sag.

18) What type of effects does the sudden increase in voltage (or) over voltage surge affect have on the power system?

Surges may create overvoltage, which can lead to spark over & flash over between phase & ground at the network's weakest point, the collapse of gaseous, solid, or liquid insulation, and the failure of spinning machinery and transformers.

19) What does "Bus Bar Protection" refer to?

The purpose of bus bar protection, as the name implies, is to safeguard the bus bar from any type of error. If a bus bar failure occurs, the feeders are disconnected and the whole supply is disrupted. The error has a number of causes such as an external product accidently falling over the bus bar, a failure of the circuit breakers, or a breakdown of the support insulators. The following are the most popular bus zone protection schemes

- Back-up protection
- Circulating current protection
- Voltage Overvoltage protection
- Differential Overcurrent protection
- Frame leakage protection

20) What are the primary effects of the electrical faults?

The following are some of the effects of power system faults:

- The heat produced by the significant quantity of the defect might result in overheating and mechanical stress.
- There is always a risk of fire due to arcing large currents create. The fire can spread to the system component if the malfunction continues for a longer period of time.
- Additionally, overheating may shorten the life of insulation by weakening it.
- Rotating machinery linked to the system may get heated by imbalanced current and voltage.
- Since each generator is linked to the others, synchronisation is required. Unbalanced current and voltage may cause the whole system to crash, and in the worst condition, they might cause a blackout.
- Because the supply to the customers may be interrupted, it may also make the system less reliable. Additionally, a failure might harm the tools utilised in the power system network.

In order to prevent the problem mentioned above, it is essential to repair the system's problematic component.

21) What is the purpose of bundle conductor?

A bundle conductor is made up of two or more sub-conductors. It functions as a conductor for one phase. One, two, three, or four sub-conductors may be used to make up one phase. For voltages higher than 22 kV, bundle conductor is employed.

The transmission is the bundle conductor's primary function. By lowering inductance and the skin effect, it maintains the voltage and improves efficiency.

22) What is the different power system operational states?

The different states are:

Normal state

When both operational limits and load are satisfied, the system is said to be normal. The overall demand for all operational limitations must be satisfied for the system to operate in its natural condition.

Alert state

In the event that the system's security level is lower than a predetermined threshold or the degree of system disruption increases.

Emergency state

The system will enter the emergency state if the disruption is significant while it is in an alert state. Utilising corrective action, the system will either revert to its default settings or enter an alert mode.

Extremis state

If no preventative action is taken during the emergency condition, it moves to one of the two extremis states. In this condition, the control action has been executed in order to return the system to either the emergency condition or the regular state.

23) What is meant by Slack Bus?

When it pertains to electric power, Swing bus is another name for slack bus, and V bus is the term of slack bus. In order to keep the active power IPI & reactive power IQI in a system from becoming unbalanced during load flow studies, a slack bus is used in the system. It either sends out or takes in the active (or) reactive power coming into or going out of the system.

24) When Directional _Relays are employed?

The direction relay becomes operational whenever the power flows in the transmission line proceeds in a certain direction.

25) How many numbers of relays are necessary to effectively protecting a device?

A two-phase fault relay & one earth fault relay is needed for improved protection. In order to provide enough protection, devices will require both type of relays.

26) What is the purpose of a circuit breaker in an electrical power system?

The purpose of a circuit breaker in an electrical power system is to interrupt the flow of current in a circuit under abnormal conditions, such as short circuits or overloads, to protect the system and equipment from damage.

27) Define the term "Load Flow Analysis" in power systems.

Load Flow Analysis, also known as power flow analysis, is a numerical technique used to determine the steady-state operating conditions of an electrical power system. It calculates the voltages, currents, and power flows in the network to ensure that power generation matches load demand while maintaining system constraints.

28) What is the significance of the per-unit system in power system analysis?

The per-unit system is used to normalize and simplify the analysis of power systems by expressing all quantities (voltage, current, power) in per-unit values relative to a base value. This allows for easy comparison and analysis of different components and systems without the need to consider absolute units.

29) Explain the difference between a transmission line and a distribution line in an electrical power system.

Transmission lines are responsible for carrying bulk electrical power from power generation sources (e.g., power plants) over long distances to substations. Distribution lines, on the other hand, distribute power from substations to end-users, such as homes and businesses, over shorter distances.

30) What is reactive power, and why is it important in power systems?

Reactive power is the power associated with the exchange of energy between inductive and capacitive components in a power system. It does not perform useful work but is essential for maintaining voltage levels and system stability. Proper control of reactive power is crucial for efficient power transmission and distribution.

31) Define the "voltage regulation" of a power transformer.

Voltage regulation refers to the ability of a power transformer to maintain a stable output voltage under varying load conditions. It is expressed as a percentage and is calculated as the change in output voltage from no-load to full-load conditions relative to the no-load voltage.

32) What is a substation in an electrical power system, and what are its primary functions?

A substation is a key component in an electrical power system responsible for transforming and distributing electrical energy. Its primary functions include voltage transformation, protection, control, and the distribution of power to different feeders or lines.

33) Explain the concept of fault current in a power system.

Fault current is the current that flows in an electrical circuit when a fault (such as a short circuit or ground fault) occurs. It is a critical parameter in power system protection and must be controlled to prevent damage to equipment and ensure safety.

34) What is a synchronous generator, and how does it differ from an asynchronous generator (induction generator) in terms of operation and characteristics?

A synchronous generator is a type of electrical generator that produces electricity at a constant frequency synchronized with the grid. It operates at a fixed speed and requires a prime mover (such as a steam turbine or diesel engine) to maintain synchronization. An asynchronous generator, or induction generator, doesn't have a fixed speed and is inherently asynchronous with the grid. It doesn't require a prime mover to maintain synchronization.

35) Describe the purpose and operation of a relay in a power system protection scheme.

Relays are protective devices used in power systems to detect abnormal conditions, such as overcurrent, overvoltage, and fault currents. When a fault or abnormal condition is detected, the relay sends a signal to trip circuit breakers, disconnecting the faulty part of the system to prevent further damage and maintain system reliability.

36) What is load shedding in the context of power systems, and why is it implemented during system emergencies?

Load shedding is the controlled reduction or disconnection of power supply to certain areas or customers during emergencies when the power system is under stress or at risk of instability. It is implemented to prevent widespread blackouts by reducing the overall load on the system and allowing for its stabilization.

37) Explain the concept of "power factor" in electrical systems and its importance in power quality.

Power factor is a measure of how effectively electrical power is being converted into useful work in an AC circuit. It is the ratio of real power (in watts) to apparent power (in volt-amperes). A high power factor indicates efficient power usage, while a low power factor can lead to increased losses and decreased system efficiency. Power factor correction is often employed to improve power quality.

38)What is a "bus" in the context of a power system's single-line diagram, and what are the different types of buses commonly used?

In a power system's single-line diagram, a bus represents a point at which multiple electrical components or devices are connected. Common types of buses in power systems include the generator bus (G-bus), load bus (PQ-bus), and the slack or swing bus (PV-bus). Each bus type has specific characteristics and is used to model different components of the power system.

39) What is the significance of a "fault analysis" in power systems, and what types of faults are commonly analyzed?

Fault analysis is essential in power systems to understand the impact of faults (short circuits or other abnormalities) on system components and operations. Common fault types include three-phase faults, line-to-line faults, and single -line-to-ground faults.

40) Define "load factor" and "diversity factor" in the context of power system planning and design.

The load factor is the ratio of the average load to the maximum load on a system over a specified time period. Diversity factor represents the ratio of the sum of individual loads to the maximum demand. These factors help in sizing and designing power system components for efficient operation.

41) Explain the operation and advantages of High Voltage Direct Current (HVDC) transmission systems in power transmission.

HVDC systems transmit electrical power over long distances with lower losses compared to AC transmission. They convert AC to DC at the sending end, transmit the power, and then convert it back to AC at the receiving end. Advantages include reduced losses, increased transmission capacity, and improved control of power flow.

42) What is a "protective relay" in a power system, and how does it work to protect the system from faults?

A protective relay is an essential device that monitors electrical quantities and trips circuit breakers when abnormal conditions, such as overcurrent, overvoltage, or short circuits, are detected. It safeguards the system by isolating the faulty part and preventing further damage.

43)Describe the concept of "voltage sag" and its impact on sensitive electrical equipment in industrial settings.

A voltage sag is a temporary and sudden drop in voltage on an electrical network, often caused by events like motor startups or faults. Voltage sags can disrupt sensitive equipment, leading to malfunctions or damage. Voltage sag mitigation strategies, such as using voltage regulators or uninterruptible power supplies (UPS), are employed to protect equipment.

44) What is the concept of "load frequency control" (LFC) in power systems, and why is it important?

Load Frequency Control (LFC) is a mechanism used to maintain the balance between power generation and load demand in real-time. It continuously adjusts the generation to match load changes, ensuring the system frequency remains stable. LFC is crucial for grid reliability and maintaining the power system's overall integrity.

45) Explain the purpose and operation of a "power factor correction" system in industrial power distribution.

Power factor correction systems are used to improve the power factor of a load, making it closer to unity (1.0). These systems use capacitors to provide reactive power, which offsets the inductive component of the load, reducing losses and improving overall system efficiency.

46) What is the difference between a "radial distribution system" and a "ring distribution system" in electrical power distribution?

A radial distribution system has a single point of supply, and power flows in one direction from the source to the loads. In contrast, a ring distribution system is a closed-loop network where power can flow in either direction, providing redundancy and reliability.

47) What is the "skin effect" in power transmission lines, and how does it affect the behavior of high-frequency alternating current?

The skin effect is the tendency of high-frequency AC current to flow primarily near the surface of a conductor. This phenomenon results in increased effective resistance for high-frequency AC, which leads to higher losses and reduced conductor efficiency.

48) Explain the concept of "fault clearing time" in the context of power system protection and its importance.

Answer: Fault clearing time refers to the time it takes for a protective device, such as a circuit breaker or relay, to detect a fault, isolate the faulty portion of the system, and restore normal operation. Short fault clearing times are crucial to minimizing damage and maintaining system stability during faults.

49) What is the concept of "load shedding" in power system control, and under what circumstances is it implemented?

Load shedding is the controlled and temporary reduction of power supply to certain areas or customers during emergencies when the power system is under stress or at risk of instability. It is implemented to prevent widespread blackouts and to balance the supply and demand of electrical power.

50) Describe the function of a "busbar" in an electrical substation, and explain its importance in the power distribution system.

A bus bar is a conductor or a set of conductors in an electrical substation that connects various components such as circuit breakers, transformers, and transmission lines. It plays a central role in the distribution and transfer of power, enabling the safe and efficient operation of the substation.

51) What is the "maximum power transfer theorem" in electrical circuits, and how does it relate to power system analysis?

The maximum power transfer theorem states that for a resistive load in an AC circuit, the load will receive maximum power when its impedance is equal to the complex conjugate of the source impedance. While it is commonly applied in circuit analysis, its relevance in power systems varies depending on the specific context.

52) Explain the concept of "relay coordination" in power system protection and its role in maintaining system reliability.

Relay coordination involves setting protective relays at different locations in the power system to ensure that the relay nearest a fault operates faster than others farther away. Proper coordination prevents unnecessary tripping of healthy components and isolates faults effectively to maintain system reliability.

53) Define "power quality" in the context of electrical power systems, and list some common power quality issues that can affect industrial operations.

Power quality refers to the cleanliness, stability, and reliability of the electrical power supplied to a facility. Common power quality issues include voltage sags, voltage swells, harmonics, and transients. These issues can disrupt industrial operations and damage sensitive equipment.

Power Systems Interview Questions & Answers-Set 5

1) What are the sources of reactive power? How it is controlled?

The sources of reactive power are generators, capacitors, and reactors. These are controlled by field excitation.

2) Give some excitation system amplifier.

The excitation system amplifiers are,

1. Magnetic amplifier
2. Rotating amplifier
3. Modern electronic amplifier.

3) When is feedback stability compensation used?

High loop gain is needed for static accuracy but this causes undesirable dynamic response, possibly instability. This conflicting situation is resolved by adding feedback stabling compensation to the AVR loop.

4) Give the characteristics of line compensators?

The characteristics of line compensators are,

1. Ferranti effect is minimized.
2. Under excited operation of synchronous generator is not required.

5) What is known as bank of capacitors? How it is adjusted?

When a number of capacitors are connected in parallel to get the desired capacitance, it is known as bank of capacitors. These can be adjusted in steps by switching (mechanical).

6) What is the disadvantage of switched capacitors are employed for compensation?

When switched capacitors are employed for compensation, these should be disconnected immediately under light load conditions to avoid excessive voltage rise and Ferro resonance in presence of transformers.

7) What are the effects of capacitor in series compensation circuit?

The effects of capacitor in series compensation circuit are,

- Voltage drop in the line reduces.
- Prevents voltage collapse.
- Steady state power transfer increases.
- Transient stability limit increases.

8) What kind of capacitors used in shunt compensator?

The capacitors used in shunt compensator are,

Static Var Compensator (SVC) : These are banks of capacitors (sometimes inductors also for use under light load conditions).

9) What is synchronous condenser?

It is a synchronous motor running at no-load and having excitation adjustable over a wide range. It feeds positive VARs into the line under overexcited conditions and negative VARs when under excited.

10) Write about Static VAR Compensator (SVC).

These comprise capacitor bank fixed or switched or fixed capacitor bank and switched reactor bank in parallel. These compensators draw reactive power from the line thereby regulating voltage, improve stability (steady state and dynamic), control overvoltage and reduce voltage and current unbalances. In HVDC application these compensators provide the required reactive power and damp out sub harmonic oscillations.

11) What is Static VAR Switches or Systems?

Static VAR compensators use switching for var control. These are also called static VAR switches or systems. It means that terminology wise

SVC=SVS. And we will use these interchangeably.

12) Give some of the Static compensators schemes. a. Saturated reactor

1. Thyristor- Controlled Reactor (TCR)
2. Thyristor Switched capacitor (TSC)
3. Combined TCR and TSC compensator.

13)What is tap changing transformers?

All power transformers and many distribution transformers have taps in one or more windings for changing the turn's ratio. It is called tap changing transformers.

14) Write the types of tape changing transformers. a. Off- load tap changing transformers.

1. Tap changing under load transformers.

15) What is the use of off-load tap changer and TCUL?

The off- load tap changers are used when it is expected that the ratio will need to be changed only infrequently, because of load growth or some seasonal change.

TCUL is used when changes in ratio may be frequent or when it is undesirably to de-energize the transformer to change the tap.

16) Define economic dispatch problem?

The objective of economic dispatch problem is to minimize the operating cost of active power generation.

17) Define incremental cost?

The rate of change of fuel cost with active power generation is called incremental cost. Write the load balance equation? Pg- pd- pl=0.

18) Define base point?

The present operating point of the system is called base point.

19) Define participation factor?

The change in generation required to meet power demand is called as participation factor.

20) Define hydrothermal scheduling problem?

The objective is to minimize the thermal generation cost with the constraints of water availability.

21) Define Unit commitment?

Commitment of minimum generator to meet the required demand. Unit commitment (UC) is a popular problem in electric power system that aims at minimizing the total cost of power generation in a specific period, by defining an adequate scheduling of the generating units.

22) Define spinning reserve?

It is the term describe the total amount of generation availability from all units synchronized on the system.

23) What is meant by scheduled reserve?

These include quick start diesel turbine units as well as most hydro units and pumped storage hydro units that can be brought online, synchronized and brought up to full capacity quickly.

24) What are the thermal unit constraint?

Minimum up time, minimum down time crew constraints.

25) Define minimum up time?

Once the unit is running, it should not be turned off immediately.

26) Define minimum down time?

Once the unit is committed, there is a minimum time before it can be recommended.

27)Define crew constraints?

If a plant consists of two (or) more units, all the units cannot be turned on at the same time since there are not enough crew members to attend both units while starting up.

28) What are the two approaches to treat a thermal unit to operating temperature?

The first allow the unit boiler to cool down and then heat backup to operating temperature in time for a scheduled turn on. The second requires that sufficient energy be input to the boiler to just maintain operating temperature.

29) What are the techniques for the solution of the unit commitment problem?

Priority list method dynamic programming Lagrange relation

30) What are the assumptions made in dynamic programming problem?

A state consists of an array of units with specified units operating and the rest of the time. The start-up cost of a unit is independent of the time it has been offline. There are no costs for shutting down the units.

31) Define long range hydro scheduling problem?

The problem involves the long range of water availability and scheduling of reservoir water releases. For an interval of time that depends on the reservoir capacities.

32) What are the optimization technique for long range hydro scheduling problem?

Dynamic programming composite hydraulic simulation methods statistical production cost.

33) Define short range hydro scheduling problem?

It involves the hour by hour scheduling of all generators on a system to achieve minimum production condition for the given time period.

34) Define system blackout problem?

If any event occurs on a system that leaves it operating with limits violated, the event may be followed by a series of further actions that switch other equipment out of service. If the process of cascading failures continues, the entire system of it may completely collapse. This is referred as system blackout.

35) What is meant by cascading outages?

If one of the remaining lines is now too heavily loaded, it may open due to relay action, thereby causing even more load on the remaining lines. This type of process is often termed as cascading outage.

36) What are the functions of control centre?

System monitoring contingency analysis security constrained optimal power flow.

37) What is the function of system monitoring?

System monitoring provides up to date information about the power system.

38) Define scada system?

It stands for supervisory control and data acquisition system, allows a few operators to monitor the generation and high voltage transmission systems and to take action to correct overloads.

39) What are the states of power system?

Normal state alert mode contingency mode emergency mode. Define normal mode? The system is in secure even the occurrence of all possible outages has been simulated the system remain secure is called normal mode.

40) Define alert mode?

The occurrence of all possible outages the system does not remain in the secure is called alert mode.

41) What are the distribution factors?

Line outage distribution factor, generation outage distribution factor.

42) Define state estimation?

State estimation is the process of assigning a value to an unknown system state variable based on measurements from that system according to some criteria.

43) Define max. likelihood criterion?

The objective is to maximize the probability that estimate the state variable x, is the true value of the state variable vector (i.e., to maximize the P(x)=x).

44) Define weighted least-squares criterion?

The objective is to minimize the sum of the squares of the weighted deviations of the estimated measurements z, from the actual measurement.

45) Define minimum variance criterion?

The objective is to minimize the expected value of the squares of the deviations of the estimated components of the state variable vector from the corresponding components of the true state variable vector.

46) Define must run constraint?

Some units are given a must run status during certain times of the year for reason of voltage support on the transmission network.

47) Define fuel constraints?

A system in which some units have limited fuel or else have constraints that require them to burn a specified amount of fuel in a given time.

48) What are the assumptions made in priority list method?

No load cost are zero unit input-output characteristics are linear between zero output and full load there are no other restrictions start-up cost are affixed amount.

49) State the advantages of forward DP approach?

If the start-up cost of a unit is a function of the unit is a function of the time it has been offline, then a forward dynamic program approach is more suitable since the previous history of the unit can be computed at each stage.

50) State the disadvantage of dynamic programming method?

It has the necessity of forcing the dynamic programming solution to search over a small number of commitment states to reduce the number of combinations that must be tested in each period.

51) What are the known values in short term hydro scheduling problem?

The load, hydraulic inflows & unit availabilities are assumed known. What is meant by telemetry system? The states of the system were measured and transmitted to a control centre by means of telemetry system.

52) What are the functions of security constraints optimal power flow?

In this function, contingency analysis is combined with an optimal power flow which seeks to make changes to the optimal dispatch of generation. As well as other adjustments, so that when a security analysis is run, no contingency result in violations.

53) Define the state of optimal dispatch?

This is the state that the power system is in prior to any contingency. It is optimal with respect to economic operation but may not be secure.

54) Define post contingency?

This is the state of the power system after a contingency has occurred. Define secure dispatch? This is state of the power system with no contingency outages, but with correction to the operating parameters to account for security violations.

55) What are the priorities for operation of modern power system?

Operate the system in such a way that power is delivered reliably. Within the constraints placed on the system operation by reliability considerations, the system will be operated most economically.

56) What is meant by linear sensitivity factor?

Many outages become very difficult to solve if it is desired to present the results quickly. Easiest way to provide quick calculation of possible overloads is linear sensitivity factors.

57) What are linear sensitivity factors?

Generation shift factors line outage distribution factors.

58) What is the uses of line distribution factor?

It is used to apply to the testing for overloads when transmission circuits are lost.

60) What is meant by external equivalencing?

In order to simplify the calculations and memory storage the system is sub divided into 3 sub-systems called as external equivalencing.

Power Systems Interview Questions and Answers-Set 6

Q.1. What is restriking voltage?

Answer: The transient voltage which appears across the breaker contacts at the instant of arc extinction is known as the restriking voltage.

Q.2. How the voltage of a particular bus can be regulated in a power system?

Answer: The voltage of a particular bus is regulated by controlling the reactive power of the bus. If the reactive power generated is greater than consumed, the voltage goes up and vice-versa.

Q.3. What is Ferranti effect?

Answer: When a long line is operating under no load or light load condition, the receiving end voltage is greater than the sending end voltage. This is known as Ferranti effect.

Q.4. What do you mean by swing equation?

Answer: The equation describing the relative motion of rotor (load angle δ) with respect to the stator field as a function of time is known as swing equation.

Q.5. What is the good effect of corona on overhead lines?

Answer: Corona, is helpful in one respect, namely, it reduces the effect of surges and acts as a relief value for them. This is so because the surges are partially dissipated as corona.

Q.6. What do you mean by critical clearing time of a fault in a power system?

Answer: The critical clearing time is the maximum elapsed time from the intimation of the fault until its isolation such that the power system is transiently stable. So, critical clearance time of a fault is related to transient stability limit.

Q.7. For which type of motors, is the equal-area criterion for stability applicable?

Answer: Three-phase synchronous motor.

Q.8. What do you mean by surge impedance loading of transmission line?

Answer: A transmission line may be considered as generating capacitive reactive volt-amperes in its shunt capacitance and consuming inductive volt-amperes in its series inductance. The load at which the inductive and capacitive reactive volt-amperes are equal and opposite is called surge impedance loading (SIL) or natural load of the line.

Q.9. What do you mean by equal area criterion for stability?

Answer: According to equal area criterion, the system is stable if the area under Pa (accelerating power) – δ curve reduces to zero at some value of δ. In other words, the positive (accelerating) area under Pa – δ curve must be equal the negative (decelerating) area.

Q.10. What is the purpose of grading ring?

Answer: Grading ring serves two purposes:

- Equalization of voltage drop across the units.
- When used with arcing horn it protects the insulator string from flashover whenever an over voltage appears between the power structure and the power conductor.

Q.11. What is the main objective of load frequency controller in a power system?

Answer: Using load frequency controller, the change in frequency and the tie-line real power are sensed which is a measure of the change in rotor angle.

Q.12. What is low inductive current chopping problem in circuit breakers?

Answer: When low inductive current is being interrupted and the arc quenching force of the circuit breaker is more than necessary to interrupt a low magnitude of current, the current will be interrupted before its natural zero instant. In such a situation, the energy stored in the magnetic field appears in the form of high voltage across the stray capacitance, which will cause restriking of the arc.

Q.**13. When relay is said to be "over-reach"?**

Answer: A relay is said to be "over-reach" when it operates at a current which is lower than its setting.

Q.14. In which context, the equal area criterion in power systems is used?

Answer: Equal area criterion in power systems is used in the context of stability of a machine connected to infinite bus bar.

- For one machine system and infinite bus bar this method is employed.

This method is applicable to any two machine system. This method is not applicable to multi machine system directly.

Q.15. What do you mean by recovery voltage?

Answer: The power frequency r.m.s voltage that appears across the breaker contacts after the transient oscillations die out and final excitation of arc has resulted in all the poles is called the recovery voltage.

Q.16. How corona loss in an EHV line is reduced by the use of bundle conductors?

Answer: A bundle conductor is a conductor made up of two or more sub-conductors and is used as one phase conductor. The reactance of the bundle conductors is reduced because the self GMD of the conductors is increased.

By bundling the conductors, the self GMD of the conductors is increased thereby; the critical disruptive voltage is increased and hence corona loss is reduced.

Q.17. What do you mean by breaking capacity of a circuit breaker?

Answer: The breaking capacity of a breaker is the product of the breaking current and the recovery voltage.

Q.18. Why is one of the buses taken as slack bus in load flow studies?

Answer: In a power system there are mainly two types of buses: load and generator buses. The power injection is positive for generator buses and is negative for load buses. The losses remain unknown until the load flow solution is complete.

It is for this reason that generally one of the generator buses is made to take the additional real power to supply transmission losses. That is why this type of bus is also known as the slack or swing bus.

Q.19. Which type of circuit breakers is generally used in railway electrification?

Answer: Air blast circuit breaker is generally used in railway electrification.

Q.20. What do you mean by current chopping in air blast circuit breakers?

Answer: It is the phenomenon of current interruption before the natural current zero is reached. This results in the production of high voltage transient across the contacts of the circuit breakers.

Q.21. What is the difference between type tests and routine tests of circuit breakers?

Answer: Routine tests are performed on every piece of circuit breaker in the premises of the manufacturer. The purpose of the routine tests is to confirm the proper functioning of a circuit breaker.

Type tests are performed in a high voltage laboratory, such tests are performed on sample piece of circuit breaker of each type confirm their characteristics and rated capacities according to their design. These tests are not performed on every piece of circuit breaker.

Q.22. What do you mean by proximity effect?

Answer: The alternating magnetic flux in a conductor caused by the current flowing in a neighbouring conductor gives rise to circulating currents which cause an apparent increase in the resistance of a conductor. This phenomenon is called proximity effect.

Q.23. Why it is desirable to have a high power factor of the system in case of HVDC transmission?

Answer: In case of HVDC transmission it is desirable to have a high power factor of the system for the following reasons –

- For a given current and voltage of the thyristor and transformers, the power rating of the converters is high.
- The stresses on the thyristor and damping circuits are reduced.

- For the same power to be transmitted the current rating of the system is reduced and also the copper losses in the ac lines are reduced.
- In the ac lines the voltage drop is reduced.

Q.24. State Kelvin's Law.

Answer: It states that, the most economical conductor size is one for which annual cost of energy loss is equal to annual interest and depreciation on the capital investment of the conductor material. This is known as Kelvin's Law.

Q.25. What is radio interference?

Answer: The corona discharge produces the radiations which may introduce noise signals in the communication lines, carrier signal, radio and television receivers, navigation signals etc. such noise signals which adversely affects the wireless signals, produced by corona is called radio interference.

Q.26. What are the properties of insulators?

Answer: The insulators must have the following properties –

- The main function of the insulators is to resist any leakage current. Thus the insulators must have very high insulation resistance.
- The insulators must be free from internal impurities such as holes, cracks, laminations etc. This reduces the permittivity of the insulators.
- The dielectric strength of the insulators must be very high.
- To have high dielectric strength, the relative permittivity of the insulating material should be very high.
- The insulating material should be non-porous.
- The insulators should not be affected by the changes in the temperature.

Q.27. How dielectric power factor vary with temperature?

Answer: The variation roughly follows a V shape; it decreases with increase in temperature to a minimum value and rises again with increase of temperature. The minimum point lies somewhere between 30 degrees and 60 degrees Celsius depending upon the type of impregnating compound.

Q.28. What is the use of stringing chart?

Answer: Stringing chart is useful for finding the sag in the conductor.

Q.29. What is "expanded ACSR"?

Answer: "Expanded ACSR" are conductor composed of filler between the inner steel and the outer aluminium strands to increase the overall diameter of the conductor.

Q.30. How sheath losses occur?

Answer: When single core cables are useful for a.c transmissions, the current flowing through the core of the cable gives rise to a pulsating magnetic field which when links the sheath, induces voltage in it. This induced voltage sets up currents under certain conditions in the sheaths and these results in sheath losses.

Q.31. What are the advantages of neutral grounding?

Answer: The advantages of neutral grounding are –

- Voltages of the phases are limited to phase to ground voltages.
- The high voltages due to arcing grounds or transient line to ground faults are eliminated.
- Sensitive protective relays against line to ground faults can be used.
- The over voltages due to lightning are discharged to ground, otherwise there will be positive reflection at the isolated neutral of the system.

Q.32. What are the methods of neutral grounding?

Answer: There are various methods of grounding the neutral of the system. They are –

- Solid grounding.
- Resistance grounding.
- Reactance grounding.
- Voltage transformer grounding.
- Zig-zag transformer grounding.

Q.33. When the Ferranti effect on long overhead lines is experienced?

Answer: In lightly loading condition because in lightly loading condition line capacitance is dominating to load reactive power requirement.

Q.34. Why mostly air blast circuit breakers are susceptible to current chopping?

Answer: Current chopping mainly occurs in air-blast circuit breakers because they retain the same extinguishing power irrespective of the magnitude of the current to be interrupted. When breaking low currents with such breakers, the powerful de-ionizing effect of air-blast causes the current fall abruptly to zero well before the natural current zero is reached.

Q.35. Define power system voltage stability.

Answer: A power system at a given operating state and subject to a given disturbance is voltage stable if voltage near loads approach posts disturbance equilibrium values. The disturbed state is within the region of attraction of the stable post disturbance equilibrium.

Q.36. What are the main insulating materials used in cables?

Answer: The main insulating materials which are in use are –

- Poly vinyl chloride (PVC).
- Paper.
- Cross linked polythene.
- Vulcanized India rubber (VIR).

Q.37. What is the difference between steady state and transient state stability of power system?

Answer: The steady state stability limit refers to maximum power transfer that is possible with small changes in power flow or gradual disturbance without losing stability.

The transient stability refers to the maximum power transfer that is possible for given amount of sudden or large changes in power disturbance without loss of stability.

Q.38. What is skin effect?

Answer: When direct current flows in the conductor, the current is uniformly distributed across the section of the conductor whereas flow of alternating current is non-uniform, with the outer filaments of the conductor carrying more current than the filament closer to the centre. This results in higher resistances to alternating current than to direct current and is commonly known as skin effect.

Q.39. What are the necessary requirements of good distribution system?

Answer: The necessary requirements of good distribution system are –

- The continuity in the power supply must be ensured. Thus system should be reliable.
- The specific consumer voltage must not vary more than the prescribed limits.
- The efficiency of the lines must be as high as possible.
- The system should be safe from consumer point of view.
- There should not be leakage.
- The lines should not be overloaded.
- The system should be economical.

Q.40. What do you understand by infinite line and infinite bus?

Answer: Infinite line – A transmission line of finite length (lossless or lossy) that is terminated at one end with an impedance equal to the characteristic impedance appears to the source like an infinitely long transmission line and produces no reflection. Infinite bus – A system bus of constant voltage and constant frequency regardless of the load is called infinite bus bar system or simply infinite bus.

Q.41. Which relay has the capability of anticipating the possible major fault in a transformer?

Answer: Buchholz relay is the gas detector relay used to protect transformers which operates when the oil level in the conservator pipe of a transformer is lowered by the accumulation of gas caused by a poor connection or by an incipient breakdown of insulation.

Q.42. Why shunt capacitors are preferred over series capacitors for improvement of power factor in distribution system?

Answer: Series capacitor compensation reduces the series impedance of the line which causes voltage drop and is the most important factor in finding the maximum power transmission capability of a line. For the same voltage boost, the reactive power capacity of a shunt capacitor is greater than that of a series capacitor. The shunt capacitor improves the power factor of the load while the series capacitor has hardly any impact on the power factor.

Q.43. What is RRRV?

Answer: RRRV stands for rate of rise of restriking voltage. It is the slope of steepest tangent to the restriking voltage curve. It is expressed in volts per microsecond. RRRV = peak value of restriking voltage / time taken to reach to peak value.

Q.44. What is the need of transposition of power transmission lines?

Answer: When the power and communication circuits run parallel to each other, interference can be reduced by transposing the conductors of the power line and the communication line. The transposition of power line neutralizes the unbalances in the capacitances of the lines that the electrically induced voltages are balanced out in a complete set of transposition.

Q.45. What are pumped storage plant?

Answer: Pumped storage plants are an special type of power plant which work as ordinary hydro power plants for part of the time and when such plants are not producing power, they can be used as pumping stations which pump water from tail race to the head race. During this time, these plants utilize power available from the grid to run the pumping set.

Q.46. What are the advantages in using bundle conductors?

Answer: The following are the advantages in using bundle conductors –

- Reduced reactance.
- Reduced voltage gradient.
- Reduced corona loss.
- Reduced radio interference.
- Reduced surge impedance.

Q.47. What is the major aspect of voltage stability?

Answer: The ability to transfer reactive power from sources to sinks during steady operating conditions is a major aspect of voltage stability.

Q.48. Which is the main relay for protecting up to 90% of the transmission line-length in the forward direction?

Answer: Mho relay is inherently a directional relay as it detects the fault only in the forward direction.

Q.49. What is the difference between symmetrical and asymmetrical breaking current?

Answer: Symmetrical breaking current – It is the rms value of a a.c component of the current in the pole at the instant of contact separation.

Asymmetrical breaking current – It is the rms value of the total current comprising the a.c and d.c components of the current in the pole at the instant of contact separation.

Q.50. What are the factors affecting corona and corona loss?

Answer: The various factors affecting corona and corona loss are –

- Electrical factors.
- Line voltage.
- Atmospheric conditions.
- Size of the conductor.
- Surface conditions.
- Number of conductors per phase.
- Spacing between conductors.
- Shape of conductors.
- Clearance from ground.
- Effect of load current.

Due to all these factors for the long transmission lines the corona loss per km of line at various points is obtained and net corona loss is obtained by taking average of all the values.

Switchgear and Protection Interview Questions and Answers- Set 7

1)What are the functions of protective relays?

To detect the fault and initiate the operation of the circuit breaker to isolate the defective element from the rest of the system, thereby protecting the system from damages consequent to the fault.

2) Give the consequences of short circuit.

Whenever a short-circuit occurs, the current flowing through the coil increases to an enormous value. If protective relays are present, a heavy current also flows through the relay coil, causing it to operate by closing its contacts. The trip circuit is then closed, the circuit breaker opens and the fault is isolated from the rest of the system. Also, a low voltage may be created which may damage systems connected to the supply.

3) Define protected zone.

Are those which are directly protected by a protective system such as relays, fuses or switchgears. If a fault occurring in a zone can be immediately detected and or isolated by a protection scheme dedicated to that particular zone.

4) What are unit system and non-unit system?

A unit protective system is one in which only faults occurring within its protected zone are isolated. Faults occurring elsewhere in the system have no influence on the operation of a unit system. A non-unit system is a protective system which is activated even when the faults are external to its protected zone.

5) What is primary protection?

It is the protection in which the fault occurring in a line will be cleared by its own relay and circuit breaker. It serves as the first line of defence.

6) What is back up protection?

Is the second line of defence, which operates if the primary protection fails to activate within a definite time delay.

7) Name the different kinds of over current relays.

Induction type non-directional over current relay, Induction type directional over current relay & current differential relay.

8) Define energizing quantity.

It refers to the current or voltage which is used to activate the relay into operation.

9) Define operating time of a relay.

It is defined as the time period extended from the occurrence of the fault through the relay detecting the fault to the operation of the relay.

10) Define resetting time of a relay.

It is defined as the time taken by the relay from the instant of isolating the fault to the moment when the fault is removed and the relay can be reset.

11) What are over and under current relays?

Overcurrent relays are those that operate when the current in a line exceeds a predetermined value. (e.g.: Induction type non-directional/directional overcurrent relay, differential overcurrent relay) whereas undercurrent relays are those which operate whenever the current in a circuit/line drops below a predetermined value. (eg: differential over-voltage relay)

12) Mention any two applications of differential relay.

Protection of generator & generator transformer unit; protection of large motors and bus bars.

13) What is biased differential bus zone reduction?

The biased beam relay is designed to respond to the differential current in terms of its fractional relation to the current flowing through the protected zone. It is essentially an over-current balanced beam relay type with an additional restraining coil. The restraining coil produces a bias force in the opposite direction to the operating force.

14) What is the need of relay coordination?

The operation of a relay should be fast and selective, ie, it should isolate the fault in the shortest possible time causing minimum disturbance to the system. Also, if a relay fails to operate, there should be sufficiently quick backup protection so that the rest of the system is protected. By coordinating relays, faults can always be isolated quickly without serious disturbance to the rest of the system.

15) Mention the short comings of Merz Price scheme of protection applied to a power transformer.

In a power transformer, currents in the primary and secondary are to be compared. As these two currents are usually different, the use of identical transformers will give differential current, and operate the relay under no-load condition. Also, there is usually a phase difference between the primary and secondary currents of three phase transformers. Even CT's of proper turn-ratio are used; the differential current may flow through the relay under normal condition.

16) What are the various faults to which a turbo alternator is likely to be subjected?

Failure of steam supply; failure of speed; overcurrent; over voltage; unbalanced loading; stator winding fault.

17) What is an under frequency relay?

An under frequency relay is one which operates when the frequency of the system (usually an alternator or transformer) falls below a certain value.

18) Define the term pilot with reference to power line protection.

Pilot wires refers to the wires that connect the CT's placed at the ends of a power transmission line as part of its protection scheme. The resistance of the pilot wires is usually less than 500 ohms.

19) Mention any two disadvantage of carrier current scheme for transmission line only.

The program time (i.e., the time taken by the carrier to reach the other end-up to .1% mile); the response time of band pass filter; capacitance phase-shift of the transmission line.

20) What are the features of directional relay?

High speed operation; high sensitivity; ability to operate at low voltages; adequate short-time thermal ratio; burden must not be excessive.

21) What are the causes of over speed and how alternators are protected from it? Sudden loss of all or major part of the load causes over-speeding in alternators.

Modern alternators are provided with mechanical centrifugal devices mounted on their driving shafts to trip the main valve of the prime mover when a dangerous over-speed occurs.

22) What are the main types of stator winding faults?

Fault between phase and ground; fault between phases and inter-turn fault involving turns of the same phase winding.

23) Give the limitations of Merz Price protection.

Since neutral earthing resistances are often used to protect circuit from earth-fault currents, it becomes impossible to protect the whole of a star-connected alternator. If an earth-fault occurs near the neutral point, the voltage may be insufficient to operate the relay. Also it is extremely difficult to find two identical CT's. In addition to this, there always an inherent phase difference between the primary and the secondary quantities and a possibility of current through the relay even when there is no fault.

24) What are the uses of Buchholz's relay?

Bucholz relay is used to give an alarm in case of incipient (slow-developing) faults in the transformer and to connect the transformer from the supply in the event of severe internal faults. It is usually used in oil immersion transformers with a rating over 750KVA.

25) What are the types of graded used in line of radial relay feeder?

Definite time relay and inverse-definite time relay.

26) What are the various faults that would affect an alternator?

(a) Stator faults

1, Phase to phase faults

2, Phase to earth faults

3, Inter turn faults

(b)1, Earth faults

2, Fault between turns

3, Loss of excitation due to fuel failure

1, Over speed

2, Loss of drive

3, Vacuum failure resulting in condenser pressure rise, resulting in shattering of the turbine low pressure casing

1, Fault on lines

2, Fault on bus bars

27) Why neutral resistor is added between neutral and earth of an alternator?

In order to limit the flow of current through neutral and earth a resistor is introduced between them.

28) What is the backup protection available for an alternator?

Overcurrent and earth fault protection is the backup protections.

29) What are faults associated with an alternator?

External fault or through fault

Internal fault

1, Short circuit in transformer winding and connection

2, Incipient or slow developing faults

30) What are the main safety devices available with transformer?

Oil level gauge, sudden pressure delay, oil temperature indicator, winding temperature indicator.

31) What are the limitations of Buchholz relay?

- Only fault below the oil level are detected.
- Mercury switch setting should be very accurate, otherwise even for vibration, there can be a false operation.
- The relay is of slow operating type, which is unsatisfactory.

32) What are the problems arising in differential protection in power transformer and how are they overcome?

- Difference in lengths of pilot wires on either sides of the relay. This is overcome by connecting adjustable resistors to pilot wires to get equipotential points on the pilot wires.
- Difference in CT ratio error difference at high values of short circuit currents that makes the relay to operate even for external or through faults. This is overcome by introducing bias coil.
- Tap changing alters the ratio of voltage and currents between HV and LV sides and the relay will sense this and act. Bias coil will solve this.

- Magnetizing inrush current appears wherever a transformer is energized on its primary side producing harmonics. No current will be seen by the secondary. CT's as there is no load in the circuit. This difference in current will actuate the differential relay. A harmonic restraining unit is added to the relay which will block it when the transformer is energized.

33) What is REF relay?

It is restricted earth fault relay. When the fault occurs very near to the neutral point of the transformer, the voltage available to drive the earth circuit is very small, which may not be sufficient to activate the relay, unless the relay is set for a very low current. Hence the zone of protection in the winding of the transformer is restricted to cover only around 85%. Hence the relay is called REF relay.

34) What is over fluxing protection in transformer?

If the turns ratio of the transformer is more than 1:1, there will be higher core loss and the capability of the transformer to withstand this is limited to a few minutes only. This phenomenon is called over fluxing.

35) Why busbar protection is needed?

- Fault level at bus bar is high
- The stability of the system is affected by the faults in the bus zone.
- A fault in the bus bar causes interruption of supply to a large portion of the system network.

36) What are the merits of carrier current protection?

Fast operation, auto re-closing possible, easy discrimination of simultaneous faults.

37) What is field suppression?

When a fault occurs in an alternator winding even though the generator circuit breaker is tripped, the fault continues to fed because EMF is induced in the generator itself. Hence the field circuit breaker is opened and stored energy in the field winding is discharged through another resistor. This method is known as field suppression.

38) What are the causes of bus zone faults?

- Failure of support insulator resulting in earth fault
- Flashover across support insulator during over voltage Heavily polluted insulator causing flashover
- Earthquake, mechanical damage etc.

39 What are the problems in bus zone differential protection?

- Large number of circuits, different current levels for different circuits for external faults.
- Saturation of CT cores due to dc component and ac component in short circuit currents. The saturation introduces ratio error.
- Sectionalizing of the bus makes circuit complicated.
- Setting of relays need a change with large load changes.

40) What is static relay?

It is a relay in which measurement or comparison of electrical quantities is made in a static network which is designed to give an output signal when a threshold condition is passed which operates a tripping device.

41) What is power swing?

During switching of lines or wrong synchronization surges of real and reactive power flowing in transmission line causes severe oscillations in the voltage and current vectors. It is represented by curves originating in load regions and traveling towards relay characteristics.

42) What is a programmable relay?

A static relay may have one or more programmable units such as microprocessors or microcomputers in its circuit.

43) What is CPMC?

It is combined protection, monitoring and control system incorporated in the static system.

44) What are the advantages of static relay over electromagnetic relay?

- Low power consumption as low as 1mW
- No moving contacts; hence associated problems of arcing, contact bounce, erosion, replacement of contacts
- No gravity effect on operation of static relays. Hence can be used in vessels i.e., ships, aircrafts etc.
- A single relay can perform several functions like over current, under voltage, single phasing protection by incorporating respective functional blocks. This is not possible in electromagnetic relays
- Static relay is compact
- Superior operating characteristics and accuracy
- Static relay can think, programmable operation is possible with static relay
- Effect of vibration is nil, hence can be used in earthquake-prone areas
- Simplified testing and servicing. Can convert even non-electrical quantities to electrical in conjunction with transducers.

45) What is resistance switching?

It is the method of connecting a resistance in parallel with the contact space(arc). The resistance reduces the restriking voltage frequency and it diverts part of the arc current. It assists the circuit breaker in interrupting the magnetizing current and capacity current.

46) What do you mean by current chopping?

When interrupting low inductive currents such as magnetizing currents of the transformer, shunt reactor, the rapid deionization of the contact space and blast effect may cause the current to be interrupted before the natural current zero. This phenomenon of interruption of the current before its natural zero is called current chopping.

47) What are the methods of capacitive switching?

- Opening of single capacitor bank

- Closing of one capacitor bank against another

48)What is an arc?

Arc is a phenomenon occurring when the two contacts of a circuit breaker separate under heavy load or fault or short circuit condition.

49) Give the two methods of arc interruption?

High resistance interruption: -the arc resistance is increased by elongating, and splitting the arc so that the arc is fully extinguished

Current zero method: -The arc is interrupted at current zero position that occurs100 times a second in case of 50Hz power system frequency in ac.

50) What is restriking voltage?

It is the transient voltage appearing across the breaker contacts at the instant of arc being extinguished.

51) What is meant by recovery voltage?

The power frequency rms voltage appearing across the breaker contacts after the arc is extinguished and transient oscillations die out is called recovery voltage.

52) What is RRRV?

It is the rate of rise of restriking voltage, expressed in volts per microsecond. It is closely associated with natural frequency of oscillation.

53) What is circuit breaker?

It is a piece of equipment used to break a circuit automatically under fault conditions. It breaks a circuit either manually or by remote control under normal conditions and under fault conditions.

54) Write the classification of circuit breakers based on the medium used for arc extinction?

- Air break circuit breaker Oil circuit breaker
- Minimum oil circuit breaker Air blast circuit breaker
- SF6 circuit breaker
- Vacuum circuit breaker

55) What is the main problem of the circuit breaker?

When the contacts of the breaker are separated, an arc is struck between them. This arc delays the current interruption process and also generates enormous heat which may cause damage to the system or to the breaker itself. This is the main problem.

56) What are demerits of MOCB?

- Short contact life
- Frequent maintenance Possibility of explosion
- Larger arcing time for small currents Prone to restricts

57) What are the advantages of oil as arc quenching medium?

- It absorbs the arc energy to decompose the oil into gases, which have excellent cooling properties
- It acts as an insulator and permits smaller clearance between line conductors and earthed components

58) What are the hazards imposed by oil when it is used as an arc quenching medium?

There is a risk of fire since it is inflammable. It may form an explosive mixture with arc. So oil is preferred as an arc quenching medium.

59) What are the advantages of MOCB over a bulk oil circuit breaker?

- It requires lesser quantity of oil
- It requires smaller space
- There is a reduced risk of fire
- Maintenance problem are reduced

60) What are the disadvantages of MOCB over a bulk oil circuit breaker?

- The degree of carbonization is increased due to smaller quantity of oil
- There is difficulty of removing the gases from the contact space in time
- The dielectric strength of the oil deteriorates rapidly due to high degree of carbonization.

61) What are the types of air blast circuit breaker?

1. Arial-blast type
2. Cross blast Radial-blast

62) What are the advantages of air blast circuit breaker over oil circuit breaker?

- The risk of fire is diminished
- The arcing time is very small due to rapid buildup of dielectric strength between contacts
- The arcing products are completely removed by the blast whereas oil deteriorates with successive operations

63) What are the demerits of using oil as an arc quenching medium?

- The air has relatively inferior arc quenching properties
- The air blast circuit breakers are very sensitive to variations in the rate of rise of restriking voltage
- Maintenance is required for the compression plant which supplies the air blast

64) What is meant by electro negativity of SF6 gas?

SF6 has high affinity for electrons. When a free electron comes and collides with a neutral gas molecule, the electron is absorbed by the neutral gas molecule and negative ion is formed. This is called as electro negativity of SF6 gas.

65) What are the characteristic of SF6 gas?

It has good dielectric strength and excellent arc quenching property. It is inert, non-toxic, non-inflammable and heavy. At atmospheric pressure, its dielectric strength is 2.5 times that of air. At three times atmospheric pressure, its dielectric strength is equal to that of the transformer oil.

66)Write the classifications of test conducted on circuit breakers.

- Type test
- Routine test Reliability test
- Commissioning test

67) What are the indirect methods of circuit breaker testing?

- Unit test
- Synthetic test
- Substitution testing o Compensation testing o Capacitance testing

68) What are the advantages of synthetic testing methods?

- The breaker can be tested for desired transient recovery voltage and RRRV.
- Both test current and test voltage can be independently varied. This gives flexibility to the test
- The method is simple
- With this method a breaker capacity (MVA) of five time of that of the capacity of the test plant can be tested.

69) How does the over voltage surge affect the power system?

The over voltage of the power system leads to insulation breakdown of the equipment. It causes the line insulation to flash over and may also damage the nearby transformer, generators and the other equipment connected to the line.

70) What is pick up value?

It is the minimum current in the relay coil at which the relay starts to operate.

71) Define target.

It is the indicator used for showing the operation of the relay.

72) Define reach.

It is the distance up to which the relay will cover for protection.

73) Define blocking.

It means preventing the relay from tripping due to its own characteristics or due to additional relays.

74) Define an over current relay.

Relay which operates when the current ia a line exceeds a predetermined value.

75) Define an undercurrent relay?

Relays which operates whenever the current in a circuit drops below a predetermined value.

76) Mention any 2 applications of differential relays.

Protection of generator and generator-transformer unit: protection of large motors and bus bars

77) Mention the various tests carried out in a circuit breaker at HV labs.

Short circuit tests, Synthetic tests& direct tests.

78) Mention the advantages of field tests.

- The circuit breaker is tested under actual conditions like those that occur in the network.
- Special occasions like breaking of charging currents of long lines, very short line faults, interruption of small inductive currents etc… can be tested by direct testing only.

79) State the disadvantages of field tests.

- The circuit breaker can be tested at only a given rated voltage and network capacity.
- The necessity to interrupt the normal services and to test only at light load conditions.
- Extra inconvenience and expenses in installation of controlling and measuring equipment in the field.

80) Define composite testing of a circuit breaker.

In this method the breaker is first tested for its rated breaking capacity at a reduced voltage and afterwards for rated voltage at a low current. This method does not give a proper estimate of the breaker performance.

81) State the various types of earthing.

Solid earthing, resistance earthing, reactance earthing, voltage transformer earthing and zig-zag transformer earthing.

82) What are arcing grounds?

The presence of inductive and capacitive currents in the isolated neutral system leads to formation of arcs called as arcing grounds.

83) What is arc suppression coil?

A method of reactance grounding used to suppress the arc due to arcing grounds.

84) State the significance of single line to ground fault.

In single line to ground fault all the sequence networks are connected in series. All the sequence currents are equal and the fault current magnitude is three times its sequence currents.

85) What are symmetrical components?

It is a mathematical tool to resolve unbalanced components into balanced components.

86) State the three sequence components.

Positive sequence components, negative sequence components and zero sequence components.

87) Define positive sequence component.

-has 3 vectors equal in magnitude and displaced from each other by an angle 120 degrees and having the phase sequence as original vectors.

88) Define zero sequence component.

They have 3 vectors having equal magnitudes and displaced from each other by an angle zero degrees.

89) State the significance of double line fault.

It has no zero sequence component and the positive and negative sequence networks are connected in parallel.

90) Define negative sequence component.

It has 3 vectors equal in magnitude and displaced from each other by an angle 120 degrees and has the phase sequence in opposite to its original phasors.**91) State the different types of faults.**

Symmetrical faults and unsymmetrical faults and open conductor faults.

92) State the various types of unsymmetrical faults.

Line to ground, line to line and double line to ground faults

93) Mention the withstanding current in our human body.

9mA

94) State the different types of circuit breakers.

Air, oil, vacuum circuit breakers.

95) Define per unit value.

It is defined as the ratio of actual value to its base value. 96. Mention the inductance value of the Peterson's coil.

$L=1/3\omega c^2$

96) Define single line diagram.

Representation of various power system components in a single line is defined as single line diagram.

97) Differentiate between a fuse and a circuit breaker.

Fuse is a low current interrupting device. It is a copper or an aluminium wire. Circuit breaker is a high current interrupting device and it act as a switch under normal operating conditions.

98) What is circuit breaker?

A circuit breaker is an electrical safety device that protects electrical circuits from damage caused by short circuits, overloads, or ground faults.

99) How direct tests are conducted in circuit breakers?

Using a short circuit generator as the source.

Using the power utility system or network as the source.

100) What is dielectric test of a circuit breaker?

It consists of overvoltage withstand test of power frequency lightning and impulse voltages. Test are done for both internal and external insulation with switch in both open and closed conditions.

Power System Protection and Relays Questions & Answers- Set 8

1) What is protective relay?

It is an electrical device designed to initiate the isolation of a part of the electrical installation, or to operate an alarm signal, in the event of abnormal condition or a fault. In simple words relay is an electrical device that gives signal to isolation device (e.g.: Circuit Breaker) after sensing the fault and helps to isolate the fault system from the healthy electrical system.

2) What are the different relays that employed for protection of apparatus and transmission lines?

The relays that are usually employed for protection of transmission lines include

- Over current relay
- Directional relay
- Distance relay
- Under Voltage relay
- Under-frequency relay
- Thermal relay
- Differential relay
- Phase sequence relays
- pilot relays

3) How the electrical power system protection is divided?

The overall system protection is divided into

- Generator protection
- Transformer protection
- Busbar protection
- Transmission line protection and
- Feeder protection

4) How relays are connected in the power system?

The relays are connected to the power system through the current transformer (CT) or potential transformer (PT).

5) What are different types of principles of operation of electro-mechanical relays?

Electro-mechanical relays operate by two principles. Electro-magnetic attraction and electro-magnetic induction. In electromagnetic attraction relay plunger is drawn to the solenoid or an armature is attracted to the poles of the electromagnet. In case of electro-magnetic induction, principle of operation is similar to induction motor. Torque is developed by electromagnetic induction principle.

6) Action carried out by the relay and circuit breaker during fault condition?

After the relay sensing the fault condition, relay operates and close the trip coils. The effect of this will be circuit breaker operate to open the contacts.

7) What is Relay Time?

Relay time is the interval between the occurrence of the fault and the closure of the relay contacts is called relay time.

8) What is fault clearance time?

When the fault occurs relay operates and close the trip coils and circuit breaker operates and open the contacts subsequently and fault is cleared. Therefore, fault clearance time is the sum of relay operating time and circuit breaker operating time and clearing the fault

9) What is Reach?

Distance relay operates whenever the impedance seen (V/I) seen by the relay is less than the specified set value. This impedance or corresponding distance is known as reach of the relay. Reach is the limiting distance covered by the relay for protection of line. Faults beyond the distance (reach of the relay) relay will not operate and should be covered by the other relay.

10) What are the fundamental elements of relay?

Basic fundamental elements of the relay are:

- *Sensing element:* It is the measuring element measures the actuating quantity. Actuating quantity is change in current in case of over current relay
- *Comparing element:* It compares the actuating quantity with the relay pre-setting of the relay
- *Control element:* On pick up of the relay control element carryout the final switching operations such as closing the circuit to operate the circuit breaker

11) What are the good features of protective relaying?

Some of the good features for protective relaying are: Reliability, Selectivity, Sensitivity, Simplicity, Speed and economy

12) Some of the causes for relay failures?

Primary reason for relay failure to operate during faults are wrong settings, bad contacts and open circuit in the relay coil.

13) What is Relay Time?

Relay time is the interval between the occurrence of the fault and the closure of the relay contacts is called relay time.

14) What is fault clearance time?

When the fault occurs relay operates and close the trip coils and circuit breaker operates and open the contacts subsequently and fault is cleared. Therefore, fault clearance time is the sum of relay operating time and circuit breaker operating time and clearing the fault

15) What is Reach?

Distance relay operates whenever the impedance seen (V/I) seen by the relay is less than the specified set value. This impedance or corresponding distance is known as reach of the relay. Reach is the limiting distance covered by the relay for protection of line. Faults beyond the distance (reach of the relay) relay will not operate and should be covered by the other relay.

16) What are the fundamental elements of relay?

Basic fundamental elements of the relay are:

- *Sensing element:* It is the measuring element measures the actuating quantity. Actuating quantity is change in current in case of over current relay
- *Comparing element:* It compares the actuating quantity with the relay pre-setting of the relay
- *Control element:* On pick up of the relay control element carryout the final switching operations such as closing the circuit to operate the circuit breaker

11) What are the good features of protective relaying?

Some of the good features for protective relaying are: Reliability, Selectivity, Sensitivity, Simplicity, Speed and economy

12) Some of the causes for relay failures?

Primary reason for relay failure to operate during faults are wrong settings, bad contacts and open circuit in the relay coil.

2) What devices are required to give adequate protection to the motor?

1. Under-voltage release to prevent automatic restarting after a stoppage due to a drop in voltage or failure of the supply, where unexpected restarting of the motor might cause injury to an operator.
2. Overload relays for protection against excessive current in the motor windings – e.g. in the event of overload or failure of the motor.
3. Earth fault.
4. Single phase protection.

3) What provision must be made for short-circuit conditions in motor circuits?

Since overload relays are not designed to operate and clear the circuit in the event of a short-circuit. Circuit-breaker or fuse protection of sufficient breaking capacity to deal with any possible short-circuit that may occur must be provided.

4) What are the usual forms of overload relay in motor-control gear?

In small contactor starters, generally thermal relays, either of the 'solder pot' or bimetal type. With large contactors or oil switches, magnetic relays of the solenoid type with dashpots. Either type of overload relay may be used within intermediate sizes.

5) How do thermal relays work?

The bimetallic thermal relay consists of a small bimetallic strip that is heated by an element connected in series with the supply. When the current rises above a preset value, the movement of the strip releases a catch which opens the trip contacts.

In recent years more modern electronic relays are used which simulate the thermal overload. Many of these relays also incorporate a memory, i.e. simulates the temperature rise / cooling curve of the winding.

6) How does the magnetic overload relay operate?

A solenoid connected in series with the supply contains a plunger whose movement is damped by a dashpot. When the safe current is exceeded, the solenoid pulls the plunger up – disconnecting the supply. The damping provided by the dashpot prevents unwarranted tripping on short-time overloads.

7) How many overload relays are required in the control gear?

On three-phase supplies where the neutral point of the system is connected to earth, as is usually the case, three overload relays (one in each line) are necessary for complete protection.

For 2-phase 3-wire and 4-wire supplies, two overload relays are required, one in each phase line, none being connected in any neutral or earth conductor.

With single-phase motors one overload relay in any conductor except an earthed conductor or neutral.

8) What happens when one of the three lines supplying a three-phase induction motor becomes open-circuited?

The motor, if already running, will continue to run as a single-phase motor on the remaining single-phase supply. The condition is called single-phasing. If the motor is loaded to more than about 30 per cent of full load, the currents in the motor windings tend to become excessive and overheating occurs.

With one line broken, the motor will not start up and, due to the heavy standstill current, burn-out is likely unless the motor is quickly disconnected.

9) What currents flow in a single-phasing delta-connected motor?

Assuming that supply line L1 is open circuited as shown, typical line and phase currents, given as percentages of normal full-load three-phase current, at various loads will be:-

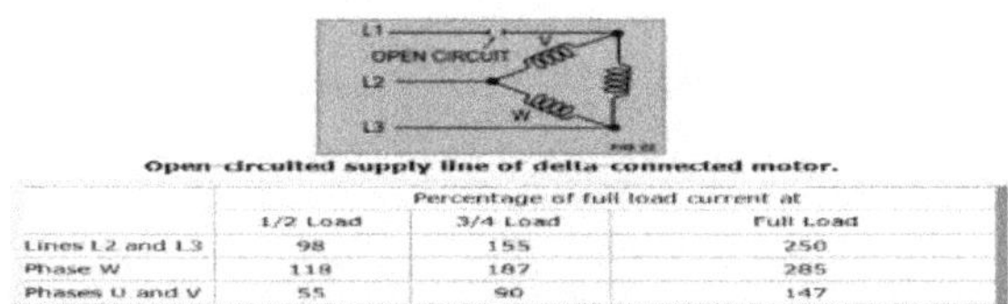

Open-circuited supply line of delta-connected motor.

	Percentage of full load current at		
	1/2 Load	3/4 Load	Full Load
Lines L2 and L3	98	155	250
Phase W	118	187	285
Phases U and V	55	90	147

Thus, phase W connected across the two operative lines carries nearly three times normal current under single-phasing conditions at full load, while phases U and V, which are in series, carry more than full-load current.

10) What currents flow in a single-phasing star-connected motor?

Assuming that line L1 is open-circuited as shown, the current flowing at full load in lines L2 and L3 and through the two phases in series will be of the order of 250 percent of normal full-load current, 155 per cent on 3/4-load and 98 per cent on 1/2-load.

11) Will normal overload relays trip on single-phasing?

If correctly set, the normal overloads will trip when the motor is fully loaded due to the rise in current passing through the closed supply lines. With a delta-connected motor partially loaded, the rise in line current may not be sufficient to operate the overload trip and one phase may became excessively overheated.

12) What special protection can be provided against single-phasing?

One method is to incorporate a combined overload and single-phase relay in the control gear. A typical relay of this type includes three overload relays with trip contacts so arranged that it will trip if the displacement of one overload element differs from that of the others.

This type of relay will operate if single-phasing occurs at or near full load with the same time delay as on overload, but at light loads, the time delay for single-phase protection is longer. Another device is a phase-failure relay in the control gear. Its principle is based on the fact that the currents in the supply lines or the voltages between them at the motor terminals are unbalanced when the motor is single-phasing.

The phase-failure relay may be of the current or voltage-operated type which trips out the line switch when one of the supply lines becomes open circuited.

13) What are the alternatives to the use of overload releases?

Direct protection against overheating or burning-out of motor windings may be built into the motor. Built-in protectors may take the form of thermostats or thermistors embedded in the end windings of the stator while the motor is under construction. These devices are sensitive to the winding temperatures and are arranged in a suitable circuit so as to cause the motor to be switched off if the windings heat up excessively.

14) How are built in thermal overload protector arranged?

On smaller motors LV mush winding motors, these detectors are embedded in the overhang of the winding. On the medium voltage motors these are placed in between bottom and top coils in the slot portion of the core.

15) How do built-in thermal overload protectors work?

Thermistors are very small semiconductor devices whose resistance changes rapidly with temperature. Three thermistors are inserted in the end-windings of the stator, one in each phase, and are connected in series. The two thermistor terminals at the motor are connected to an electronic-amplifier-control unit in the starter, through which the tripping circuit of the starter is operated. The response of the thermistors to temperature change is extremely rapid, allowing this type of protection to be effective under all motor overload conditions.

16) Resistance temperature devices (RTD)

This is a resistance which increases linearly with temperature rise. The most commonly used in motors is embedded in an epoxy glass type wedge which can be inserted between the upper and lower coils. The resistance is measured with an electronic amplifier control unit which is converted to temperature.

This unit has adjustable settings to allow for alarm and trip with contacts which are then used in the motor starter circuit.

17) Thermocouples

A thermocouple is two dissimilar metals which are joined together and with a change in temperature, creates a voltaic action. This gives out a milli-volt signal which is then measured with an electronic amplifier control unit converting the measurement to temperature.

18) When is direct-on-line starting used for three-phase squirrel-cage motors?

It is usual for small LV machines; for larger motors it is often necessary to use other methods of starting in order to avoid excessive starting currents. HV motors are usually DOL started. (since amps are low)

19) What are the connections for direct-on-line starters?

The scheme of connections is merely three line leads in and three motor leads out. Direct-on-line contactor starters are designed round the basic circuit shown. An isolating switch may be incorporated in the starter. If reversing is required, two contactors one for each rotation, are required and are interlocked so that only one can close at a time.

20) What are the connections for direct-on-line starters?

The scheme of connections is merely three line leads in and three motor leads out. Direct-on-line contactor starters are designed round the basic circuit shown. An isolating switch may be incorporated in the starter. If reversing is required, two contactors one for each rotation, are required and are interlocked so that only one can close at a time.

A hand-operated oil switch with under-voltage trip coil may be used with larger motors.

21) What methods are employed to reduce the starting current of squirrel-cage motors?

Where the starting conditions are light, the starting current can be lessened by some method of reducing the stator voltage when switching on. There are four ways of starting on reduced voltage:

1. Primary-resistance starting – introducing resistance between the supply and the stator windings.
2. Primary-reactor starting – introducing a reactor in series with the stator windings, usually connected in the star point.
3. Star-delta starting – connecting the stator windings in star for starting and in delta for running.
4. Auto-transformer starting – supplying the stator windings through tappings on an auto-transformer.

22) When is primary-resistance starting employed?

Generally, only for small motors on light-starting duty. The method is easily adjustable to suit the load and gives a smooth breakaway against low torque. If the resistance is adjustable, as in a faceplate starter, starting can be very smooth and this is useful for motors that must be started without any shock that might cause injury to the material being handled by the driven machine.

23) When is the primary reactor method of starting employed?

Mainly for high-tension motors on very light-starting load where a fairly heavy starting current can be permitted e.g. boiler-feed pumps in a large power station.

24) When is the star-delta starter used?

When the starting current has to be reduced and starting current and torque values one-third of those obtained with direct-on-line starting are suitable. It is necessary that the motor be designed to operate with the primary winding connected in delta, but with six terminals brought out to allow for connection in star during starting.

The plain star-delta method is used for small and medium-sized motors on light-starting loads, e.g. centrifugal pumps, fans having low inertia, line shafting and motor-generator sets. The Wauchope-type has the same uses but prevents the drop in speed when the stator is disconnected from the supply in changing from star to delta. Switching is done through resistances to maintain continuous line contact. This also obviates the momentary high current when switching from star to delta.

25) What are the connections for a star-delta starter?

Motors arranged for star-delta starting have six terminals – the two ends of each phase winding being brought out to terminals marked U1, V1, W1 and U2, V2, W2. These terminals are connected to similarly-marked terminals in the starter.

The basic circuit of a typical hand-operated air-break or oil-immersed starter is shown in the diagram, the incoming supply being controlled by a line contactor. With the change-over switch in the start position, the motor windings are connected in star (U1, V1 and W1 together) and in the running position in delta (U2 to W1, V2 to U1 and W2 to V1).

In starting the motor, the handle of the change-over switch is put into the start position, as indicated, and the 'start' button is pressed. This energizes the contactor coil which closes the triple-pole main switch and auxiliary switch (1). Note that the contactor coil cannot be energized unless the changeover switch has been placed in the 'start' position.

When the motor has reached full speed, which is noticeable by sound, the handle of the change-over switch is moved to the 'run' position and the 'start' button is released. The motor is now directly connected to the line.

In some star-delta starters, the overload units are by-passed in the 'start' position. A complete connection diagram of a hand-operated star-delta starter with this feature is also shown. Apart from the fact that the over-load units are brought into circuit only in the ~run~ position, the circuit is the same at the basic circuit.

A fully-automatic star-delta starter has two contactors and a triple-pole line contactor with time-delay relay between 'start' and 'run' connections.

26) When is an auto-transformer starter used?

When more flexibility is required for starting a squirrel-cage motor than is provided by the star-delta method, which is limited as far as starting torque is concerned. Auto-transformer starting permits the stator to be wound for running in star. The starting torque can be adjusted to suit the load by changing the voltage tapping on the auto-transformer. Both starting torque and current are reduced in the same proportion.

It is used for motors of medium and large size on light starting loads (e.g. centrifugal pumps, fans, compressors and mills). Up to about 75kW the simple auto-transformer starter is employed; above this, the Korndorfer connection is recommended.

27) What does the simple auto-transformer starter consist of?

The motor is started by connecting its primary to tappings on the starting transformer; then after a time delay, re-connecting direct to the supply. The winding on each limb of the auto-transformer usually has three taps, 60, 75 and 85 per cent of line voltage, but taps to give other percentages may be arranged as required. The auto-transformer may be used in conjunction with a contactor panel, or alternatively a hand-operated switch.

An auto-transformer starter consisting of a line contactor interlocked with a hand-operated change-over switch, three thermal or magnetic overload relays and an auto-transformer.

28) What are the connections for the Korndorfer system?

The simple auto-transformer starter has the disadvantage that at the instant of transition from 'start' to 'run' the supply to the motor is interrupted. This means that the insulation may be stressed by high transient voltages.

The Korndorfer method keeps the motor connected to the supply continuously by means of the connections shown in the diagram. On the first step (a), switches 1 and 2 close and the motor accelerates at a reduced voltage determined by the transformer tapping. On the second step (b), the star point of the transformer (switch 2) is opened so that the motor continues to run with part of the transformer winding in circuit. Next, this part is short-circuited by the 'run' contactor or switch (switch 3 closes) and finally the 'start' contactor or switch (1) is opened, as shown at (c).

A fully automatic starter would comprise a triple-pole line contactor, start contactor, running contactor, three single-pole overload relays, auto-transformer with a set of links for tap-changing, a suitable timer, and 'start' and 'stop' pushbuttons.

Switching sequence for auto-transformer starting by the Korndorfer method.

1. Motor at reduced voltage from transformer.
2. Motor with part of transformer winding in series.
3. Motor at full voltage.

29) What precautions should be observed when applying reduced voltage starting to a load with rising characteristic such as fans?

If the specified starting current is too low, the motor may start correctly but not run fully up to speed. The result is that on changing over to the running or full-voltage condition a very high current may be taken, thus negating the low initial current. For this reason, even with fan drives, it is not desirable to pin the starting current lower than about 200 percent of full-load current.

30) What are the initial-starting line current and motor torque when star-delta starting?

Both line current and torque are approximately one-third of the motor standstill values on full volts.

31) What are the initial starting line current and motor torque when starting with primary resistance or primary reactance?

The initial starting line current is approximately equal to: -

$$\text{Starting Current} = \frac{\text{applied voltage}}{\text{full voltage}} \times \text{standstill current with full volts}$$

The initial starting torque is approximately equal to: -

$$\text{Starting Torque} = \left(\frac{\text{applied voltage}}{\text{full voltage}}\right)^2 \times \text{standstill torque with full volts}$$

32) What are the initial-starting line current and motor torque when starting by auto-transformer?

The initial-starting line current is approximately equal to: -

$$\text{Starting Current} = 1.1 \left(\frac{\text{applied voltage}}{\text{full voltage}}\right)^2 \times \text{standstill current with full volts}$$

The factor of 1.1 in the above allows for the magnetizing current of the auto-transformer. The initial starting torque is approximately equal to: -

Starting Torque =	(	applied voltage	$)^2$	x	standstill torque with full volts
		full voltage			

33) Why are the above values of initial-starting current and torque approximate?

Because the formulae given assume for simplicity that the standstill/reactance of a motor is constant at all voltages -that the short-circuit current varies in direct proportion to the applied voltage. Owing to magnetic saturation, particularly of the slot lips, the standstill reactance tends to be less on full volts than on reduced volts so the current and torque values tend to be rather less than those obtained by the formulae given.

34) How do the various methods of starting on reduced voltage compare as regards torque per ampere?

Star-delta and auto-transformer methods have the advantage over primary resistance and primary reactor methods.

35) What mechanical methods of reducing starting current can be adopted?

The starting duty can be reduced by fitting a centrifugal or other type of clutch which only picks up the load when the motor is well up to speed.

36) What is sequence starting?

A system of starting by which several motors of similar rating are started in sequence off one starter in conjunction with interlocked switching.

37) How are slip-ring motors started?

By first switching the supply on the stator winding with all the external rotor resistance in circuit across the slip rings and then cutting out the rotor resistance progressively as the motor speeds up until finally the rotor winding is short-circuited.

38) What is the usual arrangement of connections for a hand-operated slip-ring starter?

Small slip-ring starters usually consist of a contactor for the stator circuit and a face plate-type starting resistance for the rotor circuit. The basic essentials are shown, the three wires from the stator going to slip-ring terminals R, S and T on the motor. An actual wiring diagram is also shown. The starter must be fitted with interlocks to ensure that the resistance is all-in when starting.

With a contactor controlling the stator supply, interlocking is simply effected, as shown, through electrical contacts on the arm of the rotor starter, no current reaching the contactor coil 'I' unless the arm is in the starting position. The start button must be kept depressed until all resistance has been taken out; this ensures that the motor is not accidentally left running with some of the rotor resistance still in circuit. When the operating arm of the face- plate is in the 'run' position the start button is short-circuited.

If the motor is fitted with a device designed to lift the brushes and short-circuit the slip rings when the motor is up to speed, an interlock must be arranged in the control circuit to ensure that the brush-gear is in the starting position before the stator contactor can close.

For larger motors, a stator oil switch is usual and may be used in conjunction with a liquid resistance or an oil-immersed grid resistance in the rotor circuit.

39) What are the essentials of a full-automatic stator-rotor starter?

An automatic starter would include a triple pole contactor to control the stator circuit, together with rotor-resistance grids short-circuited by the necessary number of accelerating contactors, the last of which must be continuously rated to carry the full-load rotor current. Also required are the necessary number of overload relays and timers controlling the duration of the starting period. The number of timers and accelerating contactors correspond to the number of steps of rotor resistance that are provided. A wiring diagram -of an automatic slip ring motor starter with two steps of rotor resistance is shown. Control terminals are provided for pushbutton control from one or two positions, or alternatively, for automatic control (for use with thermostat, float-switch or similar switching) with or without a try-out switch.

When the 'start' button is pressed (or the automatic switch closes), the control circuit is made through the coil of the stator contactor M. The stator contactor closes, connecting the stator to the line. At the same time the first timing relay is TR1 is energized. At this stage, the rotor is complete through the whole resistance since the accelerating contactors 2R and 3R are open. After an adjustable delay, the contacts of TR1 close, thus energizing the accelerating contactor 2R which short-circuits a portion of the rotor resistance and energizing the second timing relay TR2. When in turn the contacts of TR2 close the second and, in this case, final contactor 3R is energized and closes, short-circuiting the whole of the rotor resistance. The overload relays are in circuit during starting and running. For automatic (2-wire) remote control, hand-resetting overloads are essential.

40) How is speed control of a slip-ring motor effected?

By introducing resistance into the rotor circuit similar to a starting resistance except that the heat losses in the resistance must be dissipated continuously. Unless the duty is intermittent, all except small sizes require some means of cooling the resistors.

Grid resistances with a motor-driven fan may be used in conjunction with a drum controller. Alternative methods are oil-immersed resistances or a liquid resistance cooled by circulating water through cooling tubes.

41) What is liquid resistance?

Insulated pots filled with a resistance solution of electrolyte, e.g. caustic soda or washing soda. Plates connected to the slip rings dip into the pots and are shorted out in the full-speed position.

Liquid starters and controllers are used for large motors.

42) What is the advantage of a liquid resistance for starting purposes?

Resistance may be reduced continuously so that, with close control over the current as indicated on an ammeter, a very smooth start can be obtained.

43) What is a slip resistance?

A fixed step of rotor resistance used to limit the current taken from the supply at the instant when peak load is applied to the motor. It is often desirable to do this on press drives, guillotines, etc. As the resistance value is small, it is usual to have a conventional starter so arranged that the last step of resistance is not cut out when the starting handle is right home. This last step of resistance is continuously rated.

44) What is meant by motors in synchronous tie?

When the two slip-ring motors are required to run at the same speed, it is possible to do this by connecting their rotors together through the slip rings in conjunction with a single slip resistance. The starter for such a scheme includes a single rotor resistance, the last step of which is the continuously-rated slip resistance, and two-stator contactors, one for each motor.

In order to limit the circulating current in the event of the motors being out of phase when started, a reactance is usually inserted in the interconnecting tie. The reactor is wound in two sections, and connected so that it is non-inductive to currents flowing through each half into the slip resistance but inductive to circulating currents between rotors. This reactance also assists load sharing when the two motors are driving a common load, as for example travel motors at opposite ends of an overhead crane.

The controller gives speed control by varying resistance in series with the rotor windings and also breaks the three stator phase in the 'off' position. The moving-copper-contact rings are shown as thick horizontal lines, while the forward and reverse steps are indicated by the numbered vertical lines. The diagram below shows the connections of series limit switches when used.

45) What is meant by Tine Graded Protection?

Time Graded protection is a scheme of over current protection, in which the discrimination is incorporated i.e, the time setting of the relays is so graded that in the event of the fault, the smallest part of the system is disconnected

46) What are the main elements of current carrier protection?

The main elements of the carrier current protection are: Transmitter, Receiver, Coupling equipment and Line trap.

47) Why Merz-Price Protection is not suitable beyond 33kV?

Difficulties are experienced in balancing the secondary of the CTs and this is why Merz-Price protection is not employed beyond 33kV.

48) What types of relays are suitable for the protection of radial feeders?

Induction type IDMT relays are more suitable for protection of the radial feeders because the time current characteristics are similar in shape and in no case they cross each other at any time.

49) What is the purpose of Line trap and Coupling capacitors in carrier channels?

Line trap is an LC network inserted between the bus bar and connection of coupling capacitors to the line and tuned to resonance at the high frequency and are used to confine the carrier currents to the protected section so as to avoid interference with or from adjacent carrier current channel.

Coupling capacitors is used to connect the high frequency (carrier) equipment to one of the line conductors and simultaneously serves to isolate the carrier equipment from high power line voltage.

50) What is Unit Protection?

Unit system of protection is one in which the protection responds to the faults in the protected zone alone and it does not respond to through faults (faults beyond the protected zone). None unit systems do not have zone boundary.

Power Systems Operation and Control Interview questions- Set 10

1) What is load curve?

The curve drawn between the variations of load on the power station with reference to time is known as load curve. There are three types, Daily load curve, Monthly load curve, Yearly load curve

2) What is daily load curve?

The curve drawn between the variations of load with reference to various time period of day is known as daily load curve.

3) What is monthly load curve?

It is obtained from daily load curve. Average value of the power at a month for a different time periods are calculated and plotted in the graph which is known as monthly load curve.

4) What is yearly load curve?

It is obtained from monthly load curve which is used to find annual load factor.

5) What is connected load?

It is the sum of continuous ratings of all the equipment's connected to supply systems.

6) What is Maximum demand?

It is the greatest demand of load on the power station during a given period.

7) What is Demand factor?

It is the ratio of maximum demand to connected load. Demand factor= (max demand)/ (connected load)

8) What is Average demand?

The average of loads occurring on the power station in a given period (day or month or year) is known as average demand.

Daily avg demand = (no of units generated per day)/ (24 hours) Monthly avg demand = (no of units generated in month)/ (no of hours in a month)

Yearly avg demand = (no of units generated in a year)/ (no of hours in a year)

9) What is Load factor?

The ratio of average load to the maximum demand during a given period is known as load factor.

Load factor = (average load)/ (maximum demand)

10) What is Diversity factor?

The ratio of the sum of individual maximum demand on power station is known as diversity factor.

Diversity factor = (sum of individual maximum demand)/(maximum demand).

11) What is Capacity factor?

This is the ratio of actual energy produced to the maximum possible energy that could have been produced during a given period.

Capacity factor= (actual energy produced)/ (maximum energy that have been produced)

12) What is Plant use factor?

It is the ratio of units generated to the product of plant capacity and the number of hours for which the plant was in operation.

Units generated per annum= average load * hours in a year

13) What is Load duration curve?

When the load elements of a load curve are arranged in the order of descending magnitudes the curve then obtained is called load duration curve.

14) What is the major control loops used in large generators?

The major control loops used in large generators are 1. Automatic voltage regulator (AVR) 2. Automatic load frequency control (ALFC).

15) What is the use of secondary loop?

A slower secondary loop maintains the fine adjustment of the frequency, and also by reset action maintains proper MW interchange with other pool members. This loop is insensitive to rapid load and frequency changes but focuses instead on drift like changes which take place over periods of minutes.

16) What is the adv of AVR loop over ALFC?

AVR loop is much faster than the ALFC loop and therefore there is a tendency, for the AVR dynamics to settle down before they can make themselves felt in the slower load frequency control channel.

17) What is the difference between large and small signal analysis?

Large signal analysis is used where voltage and power may undergo sudden changes of magnitude that may approach 100 percent of operating values. Usually this type of analysis leads to differential equations of non-linear type. Small signal analysis is used when variable excursions are relatively small, typically at most a few percent of normal operating values.

18) What is the exciter?

The exciter is the main component in AVR loop. It delivers the DC power to the generator field. It must have adequate power capacity and sufficient speed of response (rise time less than 0.1 sec).

19) What is the function of AVR?

The basic role of the AVR is to provide constancy of the generator terminal voltage during normal, small and slow changes in the load.

20) Explain about static AVR loop?

In a static AVR loop, the execution power is obtained directly from the generator terminals or from the station service bus. The AC power is rectified by thyristor bridges and fed into the main generator field via slip rings. Static exciters are very fast and contribute to improved transient stability.

21) Write the static performance of AVR loop?

The AVR loop must regulate the terminal |V| to within required static accuracy limit. Have sufficient speed of response. Be stable.

22) What is the disadvantages of high loop gain? How is to be eliminated?

High loop gain is needed for static accuracy but this causes undesirable dynamic response, possibly instability. By adding series AND/OR feedback stability compensation to the AVR loop, this conflicting situation can be resolved.

23) What are the effects of generator loading in AVR loop?

Added load does not change the basic features of the AVR loop, it will however affect the values of both gain factor K_f and the field constant. High loading will make the generator work at higher magnetic saturation levels. This means smaller changes in |E| for incremental increases in i_f, translating into the reduction of K_F. the field time constant will likewise decreases as generator loading closing the armature current paths. This circumstance permits the formation of transient stator currents the existence of which yields a lower effective field induction.

24) What are the functions of ALFC?

The basic role of ALFC's is to maintain desired MW output of a generator unit and assist in controlling the frequency of large interconnection. The ALFC also helps to keep the net interchange of power between pool members at predetermined values. Control should be applied in such a fashion that highly differing response characteristics of units of various types are recognized. Also unnecessary power output changes should be kept at a minimum in order to reduce wear of control valves.

25) Specify the disadvantages of ALFC loop?

The ALFC loop will main control only during normal changes in load and frequency. It is typically unable to provide adequate control during emergency situations, when large MW imbalances occur.

26) How is the real power in a power system controlled?

The real power in a power system is being controlled by controlling the driving torque of the individual turbines of the system.

27) What is the need for large mechanical forces in speed-governing system?

Very large mechanical forces are needed to position the main valve against the high stream pressure and these forces are obtained via several stages of hydraulic amplifiers.

Protection Relays Interview Questions & Answers- Set 11

1) Where does the Negative phase sequence relay is employed?

Negative sequence relay is employed for the protection of generators and motors against unbalanced loading that may arise due to phase to phase faults.

2) What is the operation principle of the differential relay?

A differential relay operates when the phasor difference of two or more similar electrical quantities exceeds a pre-determined amount.

3) Why distance protection is preferred as primary protection compared to overcurrent protection for transmission lines?

Distance relay is superior to overcurrent protection for the protection of transmission lines.

Some of the reasons are faster protection, simpler coordination, simpler application, permanent settings without the need for readjustment, less effect of the amount of generation and fault levels, fault current magnitude, permits the high line loading.

4) Why biased differential protection is preferred over simple differential protection?

Biased differential relay is preferred because its operation is not affected by the trouble arising out of the difference in the CTs ratios for high values of external short circuit currents.

5) Where Impedance relay, Reactance relay, and Mho relays are employed?

The Impedance relay is suitable for the phase faults relaying for the lines of moderate lengths Reactance type relays are employed for the ground faults while Mho type of relays is best suited for the long transmission lines and particularly where synchronizing power surge may occur.

6) What is the percentage differential relay?

It is a differential relay where the operating current required to trip can be expressed as a percentage of load current.

7) What are the main functions of Differential Relays?

Differential Relays must have the following features:

- High-speed operation
- High sensitivity
- Adequate short circuit thermal rating
- Ability to operate with low values of voltage
- The burden must not be excessive
- There should be no voltage and current creep

8) What is meant by "Relay Settings"?

Relay settings mean the actual value of the energizing or characteristic quantity at which the relay is designed to operate under given conditions.

9) Define Plug Setting Multiplier?

Plug Setting Multiplier and is defined as the ratio of fault current in the relay coil to the pick-up value.

10) Where is the directional relay used?

Directional relay is used when graded time overload protection is applied to ring mains and interconnected networks.

11) For what type of fault does Buchholz relay is employed?

Buchholz relay provides protection only against transformer internal fault.

12) How definite time lag is achieved in attraction armature relays?

The instantaneous type attraction armature can be made a definite time lag or inverse time lag by using an oil dashpot, an air escapement chamber, a clockwork mechanism or by placing a fuse in parallel with it.

A hand-operated oil switch with under-voltage trip coil may be used with larger motors.

13) What are the functions of protective relays

To detect the fault and initiate the operation of the circuit breaker to isolate the defective element from the rest of the system, thereby protecting the system from damages consequent to the fault.

14) Give the consequences of short circuit.

Whenever a short-circuit occurs, the current flowing through the coil increases to an enormous value. If protective relays are present, a heavy current also flows through the relay coil, causing it to operate by closing its contacts. The trip circuit is then closed, the circuit breaker opens and the fault is isolated from the rest of the system. Also, a low voltage may be created which may damage systems connected to the supply.

15) Define protected zone.

Are those which are directly protected by a protective system such as relays, fuses or switchgears. If a fault occurring in a zone can be immediately detected and or isolated by a protection scheme dedicated to that particular zone.

16) What are unit system and non-unit system?

A unit protective system is one in which only faults occurring within its protected zone are isolated. Faults occurring elsewhere in the system have no influence on the operation of a unit system. A non-unit system is a protective system which is activated even when the faults are external to its protected zone.

17) What is primary protection?

It is the protection in which the fault occurring in a line will be cleared by its own relay and circuit breaker. It serves as the first line of defence.

18) What is back up protection?

Is the second line of defence, which operates if the primary protection fails to activate within a definite time delay.

19) Name the different kinds of over current relays.

Induction type non-directional over current relay, Induction type directional over current relay & current differential relay.

20)Define energizing quantity.

It refers to the current or voltage which is used to activate the relay into operation.

21) Define operating time of a relay.

It is defined as the time period extended from the occurrence of the fault through the relay detecting the fault to the operation of the relay.

22) Define resetting time of a relay.

It is defined as the time taken by the relay from the instant of isolating the fault to the moment when the fault is removed and the relay can be reset.

23) What are over and under current relays?

Overcurrent relays are those that operate when the current in a line exceeds a predetermined value. (e.g.: Induction type non-directional/directional overcurrent relay, differential overcurrent relay) whereas undercurrent relays are those which operate whenever the current in a circuit/line drops below a predetermined value. (e.g.: differential over-voltage relay)

24) Mention any two applications of differential relay.

Protection of generator & generator transformer unit; protection of large motors and bus bars.

25) What is biased differential bus zone reduction?

The biased beam relay is designed to respond to the differential current in terms of its fractional relation to the current flowing through the protected zone. It is essentially an over-current balanced beam relay type with an additional restraining coil. The restraining coil produces a bias force in the opposite direction to the operating force.

26) What is the need of relay coordination?

The operation of a relay should be fast and selective, i.e., it should isolate the fault in the shortest possible time causing minimum disturbance to the system. Also, if a relay fails to operate, there should be sufficiently quick backup protection so that the rest of the system is protected. By coordinating relays, faults can always be isolated quickly without serious disturbance to the rest of the system.

27) Mention the short comings of Merz Price scheme of protection applied to a power transformer.

In a power transformer, currents in the primary and secondary are to be compared. As these two currents are usually different, the use of identical transformers will give differential current, and operate the relay under no-load condition. Also, there is usually a phase difference between the primary and secondary currents of three phase transformers. Even CT's of proper turn-ratio are used; the differential current may flow through the relay under normal condition.

28) What are the various faults to which a turbo alternator is likely to be subjected?

Failure of steam supply; failure of speed; overcurrent; over voltage; unbalanced loading; stator winding fault.

29) What is an under frequency relay?

An under frequency relay is one which operates when the frequency of the system (usually an alternator or transformer) falls below a certain value.

30) Define the term pilot with reference to power line protection.

Pilot wires refers to the wires that connect the CT's placed at the ends of a power transmission line as part of its protection scheme. The resistance of the pilot wires is usually less than 500 ohms.

31) Mention any two disadvantage of carrier current scheme for transmission line only.

The program time (i.e., the time taken by the carrier to reach the other end-up to .1% mile); the response time of band pass filter; capacitance phase-shift of the transmission line.

32) What are the features of directional relay?

High speed operation; high sensitivity; ability to operate at low voltages; adequate short-time thermal ratio; burden must not be excessive.

33) What are the causes of over speed and how alternators are protected from it? Sudden loss of all or major part of the load causes over-speeding in alternators.

Modern alternators are provided with mechanical centrifugal devices mounted on their driving shafts to trip the main valve of the prime mover when a dangerous over-speed occurs.

34) What are the main types of stator winding faults?

Fault between phase and ground; fault between phases and inter-turn fault involving turns of the same phase winding.

35) Give the limitations of Merz Price protection.

Since neutral earthing resistances are often used to protect circuit from earth-fault currents, it becomes impossible to protect the whole of a star-connected alternator. If an earth-fault occurs near the neutral point, the voltage may be insufficient to operate the relay. Also it is extremely difficult to find two identical CT's. In addition to this, there always an inherent phase difference between the primary and the secondary quantities and a possibility of current through the relay even when there is no fault.

36) What are the uses of Buchholz's relay?

Bucholz relay is used to give an alarm in case of incipient(slow-developing) faults in the transformer and to connect the transformer from the supply in the event of severe internal faults. It is usually used in oil immersion transformers with a rating over 750KVA.

37) What are the types of graded used in line of radial relay feeder?

Definite time relay and inverse-definite time relay.

38) What are the various faults that would affect an alternator?

Stator faults

1, Phase to phase faults

2, Phase to earth faults

3, Inter turn faults

(b)1, Earth faults

2, Fault between turns

3, Loss of excitation due to fuel failure

1, Over speed

2, Loss of drive

3, Vacuum failure resulting in condenser pressure rise, resulting in shattering of the turbine low pressure casing

1, Fault on lines

2, Fault on bus bars

39) Why neutral resistor is added between neutral and earth of an alternator?

In order to limit the flow of current through neutral and earth a resistor is introduced between them.

40) What is the backup protection available for an alternator?

Overcurrent and earth fault protection is the backup protections.

41) What are faults associated with an alternator?

External fault or through fault

Internal fault

1, Short circuit in transformer winding and connection

2, Incipient or slow developing faults

42) What are the main safety devices available with transformer?

Oil level gauge, sudden pressure delay, oil temperature indicator, winding temperature indicator.

43) What are the limitations of Buchholz relay?

- Only fault below the oil level are detected.
- Mercury switch setting should be very accurate, otherwise even for vibration, there can be a false operation.
- The relay is of slow operating type, which is unsatisfactory.

44) What are the problems arising in differential protection in power transformer and how are they overcome?

- Difference in lengths of pilot wires on either sides of the relay. This is overcome by connecting adjustable resistors to pilot wires to get equipotential points on the pilot wires.
- Difference in CT ratio error difference at high values of short circuit currents that makes the relay to operate even for external or through faults. This is overcome by introducing bias coil.

- Tap changing alters the ratio of voltage and currents between HV and LV sides and the relay will sense this and act. Bias coil will solve this.

- Magnetizing inrush current appears wherever a transformer is energized on its primary side producing harmonics. No current will be seen by the secondary. CT's as there is no load in the circuit. This difference in current will actuate the differential relay. A harmonic restraining unit is added to the relay which will block it when the transformer is energized.

45) What is REF relay?

It is restricted earth fault relay. When the fault occurs very near to the neutral point of the transformer, the voltage available to drive the earth circuit is very small, which may not be sufficient to activate the relay, unless the relay is set for a very low current. Hence the zone of protection in the winding of the transformer is restricted to cover only around 85%. Hence the relay is called REF relay.

46) What is over fluxing protection in transformer?

If the turns ratio of the transformer is more than 1:1, there will be higher core loss and the capability of the transformer to withstand this is limited to a few minutes only. This phenomenon is called over fluxing.

47) Why bus bar protection is needed?

- Fault level at bus bar is high

- The stability of the system is affected by the faults in the bus zone.

- A fault in the bus bar causes interruption of supply to a large portion of the system network.

48) What are the merits of carrier current protection?

Fast operation, auto re-closing possible, easy discrimination of simultaneous faults.

49) What are the errors in CT?

(a) Accuracy errors

These errors are related to linearity or gain. For example, a CT that reads 0.5% low at 20 amps will report 19.9 amps instead of 20 amps.

(b) Phase angle errors

These errors can cause large errors in measured power and energy at lower power factors, such as 0.7 or below.

© Ratio error

This error occurs when the CT doesn't convert current precisely according to a predetermined ratio. It's caused by the difference between the primary current and the secondary current multiplied by the turns ratio.

50)What is field suppression?

When a fault occurs in an alternator winding even though the generator circuit breaker is tripped, the fault continues to fed because EMF is induced in the generator itself. Hence the field circuit breaker is opened and stored energy in the field winding is discharged through another resistor. This method is known as field suppression.

51)What are the causes of bus zone faults?

- Failure of support insulator resulting in earth fault
- Flashover across support insulator during over voltage Heavily polluted insulator causing flashover
- Earthquake, mechanical damage etc.

52) What are the problems in bus zone differential protection?

- Large number of circuits, different current levels for different circuits for external faults.

- Saturation of CT cores due to dc component and ac component in short circuit currents. The saturation introduces ratio error.

- Sectionalizing of the bus makes circuit complicated.

- Setting of relays need a change with large load changes.

53) What is static relay?

It is a relay in which measurement or comparison of electrical quantities is made in a static network which is designed to give an output signal when a threshold condition is passed which operates a tripping device.

54) What is power swing?

During switching of lines or wrong synchronization surges of real and reactive power flowing in transmission line causes severe oscillations in the voltage and current vectors. It is represented by curves originating in load regions and traveling towards relay characteristics.

55) What is a programmable relay?

A static relay may have one or more programmable units such as microprocessors or microcomputers in its circuit.

56) What is CPMC?

It is combined protection, monitoring and control system incorporated in the static system.

57) What are the advantages of static relay over electromagnetic relay?

- Low power consumption as low as 1mW

- No moving contacts; hence associated problems of arcing, contact bounce, erosion, replacement of contacts

- No gravity effect on operation of static relays. Hence can be used in vessels ie, ships, aircrafts etc.
- A single relay can perform several functions like over current, under voltage, single phasing protection by incorporating respective functional blocks. This is not possible in electromagnetic relays
- Static relay is compact
- Superior operating characteristics and accuracy
- Static relay can think, programmable operation is possible with static relay
- Effect of vibration is nil, hence can be used in earthquake-prone areas o Simplified testing and servicing. Can convert even non-electrical quantities to electrical in conjunction with transducers.

58) What is resistance switching?

It is the method of connecting a resistance in parallel with the contact space(arc). The resistance reduces the restriking voltage frequency and it diverts part of the arc current. It assists the circuit breaker in interrupting the magnetizing current and capacity current.

59) What do you mean by current chopping?

When interrupting low inductive currents such as magnetizing currents of the transformer, shunt reactor, the rapid deionization of the contact space and blast effect may cause the current to be interrupted before the natural current zero. This phenomenon of interruption of the current before its natural zero is called current chopping.

60) What are the methods of capacitive switching?

- Opening of single capacitor bank
- Closing of one capacitor bank against another

61) What is an arc?

Arc is a phenomenon occurring when the two contacts of a circuit breaker separate under heavy load or fault or short circuit condition.

62) Give the two methods of arc interruption?

1. High resistance interruption: -the arc resistance is increased by elongating, and splitting the arc so that the arc is fully extinguished

2. Current zero method: -The arc is interrupted at current zero position that occurs100 times a second in case of 50Hz power system frequency in ac.

63) What is restriking voltage?

It is the transient voltage appearing across the breaker contacts at the instant of arc being extinguished.

64) What is meant by recovery voltage?

The power frequency rms voltage appearing across the breaker contacts after the arc is extinguished and transient oscillations die out is called recovery voltage.

65) What is RRRV?

It is the rate of rise of restriking voltage, expressed in volts per microsecond. It is closely associated with natural frequency of oscillation.

66) What is circuit breaker?

It is a piece of equipment used to break a circuit automatically under fault conditions. It breaks a circuit either manually or by remote control under normal conditions and under fault conditions.

67) Write the classification of circuit breakers based on the medium used for arc extinction?

- Air break circuit breaker Oil circuit breaker

- Minimum oil circuit breaker Air blast circuit breaker
- SF6 circuit breaker
- Vacuum circuit breaker

68) What is the main problem of the circuit breaker?

When the contacts of the breaker are separated, an arc is struck between them. This arc delays the current interruption process and also generates enormous heat which may cause damage to the system or to the breaker itself. This is the main problem.

69) What are demerits of MOCB?

- Short contact life
- Frequent maintenance Possibility of explosion
- Larger arcing time for small currents Prone to restricts

70) What are the advantages of oil as arc quenching medium?

- It absorbs the arc energy to decompose the oil into gases, which have excellent cooling properties
- It acts as an insulator and permits smaller clearance between line conductors and earthed components

71) What are the hazards imposed by oil when it is used as an arc quenching medium?

There is a risk of fire since it is inflammable. It may form an explosive mixture with arc. So oil is preferred as an arc quenching medium.

72) What are the advantages of MOCB over a bulk oil circuit breaker?

- It requires lesser quantity of oil
- It requires smaller space
- There is a reduced risk of fire
- Maintenance problem are reduced

73) What are the disadvantages of MOCB over a bulk oil circuit breaker?

- The degree of carbonization is increased due to smaller quantity of oil
- There is difficulty of removing the gases from the contact space in time
- The dielectric strength of the oil deteriorates rapidly due to high degree of carbonization.

74) What are the types of air blast circuit breaker?

- Arial-blast type
- Cross blast Radial-blast

75) What are the advantages of air blast circuit breaker over oil circuit breaker?

- The risk of fire is diminished
- The arcing time is very small due to rapid build-up of dielectric strength between contacts
- The arcing products are completely removed by the blast whereas oil deteriorates with successive operations

76) What are the demerits of using oil as an arc quenching medium?

- The air has relatively inferior arc quenching properties
- The air blast circuit breakers are very sensitive to variations in the rate of rise of restriking voltage
- Maintenance is required for the compression plant which supplies the air blast

77) What is meant by electro negativity of SF6 gas?

SF6 has high affinity for electrons. When a free electron comes and collides with a neutral gas molecule, the electron is absorbed by the neutral gas molecule and negative ion is formed. This is called as electro negativity of SF6 gas.

78) What are the characteristic of SF6 gas?

It has good dielectric strength and excellent arc quenching property. It is inert, non-toxic, non-inflammable and heavy. At atmospheric pressure, its dielectric strength is 2.5 times that of air. At three times atmospheric pressure, its dielectric strength is equal to that of the transformer oil.

79) Write the classifications of test conducted on circuit breakers.

- Type test
- Routine test Reliability test
- Commissioning test

80) What are the indirect methods of circuit breaker testing?

- Unit test
- Synthetic test
- Substitution testing

- Compensation testing
- Capacitance testing

81) What are the advantages of synthetic testing methods?

- The breaker can be tested for desired transient recovery voltage and RRRV.
- Both test current and test voltage can be independently varied. This gives flexibility to the test
- The method is simple
- With this method a breaker capacity (MVA) of five time of that of the capacity of the test plant can be tested.

82) How does the over voltage surge affect the power system?

The over voltage of the power system leads to insulation breakdown of the equipment. It causes the line insulation to flash over and may also damage the nearby transformer, generators and the other equipment connected to the line.

83) What is pick up value?

It is the minimum current in the relay coil at which the relay starts to operate.

84) Define target.

It is the indicator used for showing the operation of the relay.

85) Define reach.

It is the distance up to which the relay will cover for protection.

86) Define blocking.

It means preventing the relay from tripping due to its own characteristics or due to additional relays.

87) Define an over current relay.

Relay which operates when the current ia a line exceeds a predetermined value.

88) Define an under current relay?

Relays which operates whenever the current in a circuit drops below a predetermined value.

89) Mention any 2 applications of differential relays.

Protection of generator and generator-transformer unit: protection of large motors and bus bars

90) Mention the various tests carried out in a circuit breaker at HV labs.

Short circuit tests, Synthetic tests& direct tests.

91) Mention the advantages of field tests.

- The circuit breaker is tested under actual conditions like those that occur in the network.
- Special occasions like breaking of charging currents of long lines, very short line faults, interruption of small inductive currents etc… can be tested by direct testing only.

92) State the disadvantages of field tests.

- The circuit breaker can be tested at only a given rated voltage and network capacity.
- The necessity to interrupt the normal services and to test only at light load conditions.
- Extra inconvenience and expenses in installation of controlling and measuring equipment in the field.

93) Define composite testing of a circuit breaker.

In this method the breaker is first tested for its rated breaking capacity at a reduced voltage and afterwards for rated voltage at a low current. This method does not give a proper estimate of the breaker performance.

94) State the various types of earthing.

Solid earthing, resistance earthing, reactance earthing, voltage transformer earthing and zig-zag transformer earthing.

95) What are arcing grounds?

The presence of inductive and capacitive currents in the isolated neutral system leads to formation of arcs called as arcing grounds.

96) What is arc suppression coil?

A method of reactance grounding used to suppress the arc due to arcing grounds.

97) State the significance of single line to ground fault.

In single line to ground fault all the sequence networks are connected in series. All the sequence currents are equal and the fault current magnitude is three times its sequence currents.

98) What are symmetrical components?

It is a mathematical tool to resolve unbalanced components into balanced components.

99) State the three sequence components.

Positive sequence components, negative sequence components and zero sequence components.

100) Define positive sequence component.

They have 3 vectors equal in magnitude and displaced from each other by an angle 120 degrees and having the phase sequence as original vectors.

101) Define zero sequence component.

They have 3 vectors having equal magnitudes and displaced from each other by an angle zero degrees.

102) State the significance of double line fault.

It has no zero sequence component and the positive and negative sequence networks are connected in parallel.

103) Define negative sequence component.

It has 3 vectors equal in magnitude and displaced from each other by an angle 120 degrees and has the phase sequence in opposite to its original phasors.

104) State the different types of faults.

Symmetrical faults and unsymmetrical faults and open conductor faults.

105) State the various types of unsymmetrical faults.

Line to ground, line to line and double line to ground faults

106) Mention the withstanding current in our human body.

9mA

107) State the different types of circuit breakers.

Air, oil, vacuum circuit breakers.

108) Define per unit value.

It is defined as the ratio of actual value to its base value. 96. Mention the inductance value of the peterson's coil.

$L=1/3\omega c^2$

109) Define single line diagram.

Representation of various power system components in a single line is defined as single line diagram.

110) Differentiate between a fuse and a circuit breaker.

Fuse is a low current interrupting device. It is a copper or an aluminium wire. Circuit breaker is a high current interrupting device and it act as a switch under normal operating conditions.

111) How direct tests are conducted in circuit breakers?

- Using a short circuit generator as the source.
- Using the power utility system or network as the source.

112) What is dielectric test of a circuit breaker?

It consists of overvoltage withstand test of power frequency lightning and impulse voltages. Test are done for both internal and external insulation with switch in both open and closed conditions.

www.ingramcontent.com/pod-product-compliance
Lightning Source LLC
LaVergne TN
LVHW070422170826
845679LV00035BA/1873
9798896326212